EMERGING TECH, EMERGING THREATS

A CYBERSECURITY GUIDE FOR INNOVATIVE LEADERS

By Tiago Teles (CISSP, MBA)
and
Arnaud Wiehe (CISSP, CCSP, CISM, CISA, CFE)

Dear Albert

Thanks for the amazing
collaboration over the years.

10-10-10
Publishing

Emerging Tech, Emerging Threats
www.Bookoncybersecurity.com

Copyright © 2024 Tiago Teles and Arnaud Wiehe

ISBN: 979-8-882629-49-5

References to internet websites (URLs) were accurate at the time of writing. The author and publishers are not responsible for URLs that may have expired or changed since the manuscript was prepared.

Publisher
10-10-10 Publishing
Markham, ON Canada

Tiago Teles: To Ana, for everything.

Arnaud Wiehe: To Theo for always supporting and encouraging me.

Table of Contents

Testimonials vii

Foreword ix

Chapter 1: The Imperative of Securing Emerging Technologies..1

Chapter 2: Future-Proofing Cybersecurity....................................23

Chapter 3: Artificial Intelligence and Machine Learning..............43

Chapter 4: Robots Among Us...81

Chapter 5: Internet of Things (IoT)..113

Chapter 6: Autonomous Vehicles..141

Chapter 7: Immersive Worlds, Immersive Threats.......................175

Chapter 8: Blockchain, Cryptocurrencies, NFTs,
    and Smart Contracts 197

Chapter 9: Biotechnology and Life Sciences................................229

Chapter 10: Exploring Additional Emerging Technologies.......249

Acknowledgements...279

About the Authors...285

Testimonials

Working with Tiago was an invaluable experience for our team. Tiago's extensive knowledge in the field of cybersecurity was evident from the onset. He has a unique ability to simplify complex security concepts, making them accessible to everyone in any organization. His dedication to staying ahead of emerging cybersecurity trends and threats was a great asset to everyone working with him.

Caroline Wong, Chief Strategy Officer at Cobalt and host of Humans of InfoSec Podcast

Tiago was a thoroughly engaging speaker for our attendees at the Applied IoT Security stage and delivered a clear presentation, which provided valuable key takeaways for those in the space who are seeking advice when it comes to protecting against IoT threats.

He possesses the perfect combination of technical and enterprise security expertise, which he used to effectively detail how we can best protect resources and networks within an organization.

It was a pleasure working with Tiago as an individual as well as a speaker—he is a friendly and polite person, and I would most definitely work with him again on a future event without hesitation!

Rosie Fletcher, Conference Producer at TechEx Events

I've just finished reading *The Book on Cybersecurity* by Arnaud Wiehe. It is an excellent guide to the growing cyber-threat landscape and provides practical solutions to protect against it. Arnaud has achieved the difficult balance of being understandable to the layman and insightful to the expert. Highly recommended!

Brett McDougall, National Chief Information Officer, SPAR South Africa

We were honored to have Arnaud as a speaker for the virtual day of the Economist Enterprise Metaverse Summit. He shared valuable insights on the topic of "Securing the Metaverse: The Intersection of Metaverse and Cybersecurity," and we had positive feedback from our attendees.

Helen Ponsford, Senior Programme Editor, The Economist

The presentation on the topic of "Securing the Future: The Intersection of Future Technologies and Cybersecurity" has not only given the attendees a full retrospective of consumer technologies over the years, but it also juxtaposed it with the present and future technologies and innovations. A very insightful, informative, and engaging keynote that we and our audience have experienced and learned from. Your enthusiasm for sharing your knowledge is influential in a business setting.

Dennis Torrepalma, Head Event Management Operations

Foreword

In an era where technology evolves at incredible speed, the challenge of securing these technologies is significant. *Emerging Tech, Emerging Threats* is an essential guide for innovative leaders navigating the complex world of modern cyber threats. I believe that to secure emerging technology, security leaders must embrace and use new technology as early adopters to implement innovative security measures. I believe you can't secure new technology with old technology. This book is therefore not just timely, it is a call to action for proactive, informed cybersecurity strategies and controls in the face of rapidly advancing technologies.

This book provides business leaders and innovators with the vital information needed to navigate the complexities of a digitally dependent era. *Emerging Tech, Emerging Threats* stands out not just for the expertise it encapsulates, but for its approachable narrative. Tiago and Arnaud adeptly distill complex concepts into comprehensible insights, making the subject accessible to business leaders, technology innovators, and even those new to the cybersecurity domain.

What sets this book apart is its ability to unravel the complexities of cybersecurity for emerging technologies, making the subject comprehensible and accessible. Whether you aim to develop or launch emerging technologies securely, or guide your organization toward stronger cybersecurity postures, this well-paced and positive book is an invaluable tool.

In these pages, you'll find a blend of case studies, real-world examples, and theoretical insights. The book meticulously covers a spectrum of emerging technologies-from artificial intelligence and the Internet of Things to blockchain and beyond-offering a panoramic view of the current cybersecurity landscape. It also doesn't shy away from discussing the potential future scenarios and the preparedness required to face them.

Moreover, Tiago and Arnaud's narrative transcends the technical. It delves into the ethical, legal, and societal implications of cybersecurity, making it an essential read for anyone who aspires to lead responsibly in the digital age.

I highly recommend *Emerging Tech, Emerging Threats* as a fundamental resource for understanding and countering the cybersecurity challenges of today and tomorrow. Whether you're a C-suite executive, a tech entrepreneur, a policy maker, or simply an enthusiast keen to understand the intersection of technology and security, this book is tailored for you. Immerse yourself in its pages; the knowledge you will gain is your best defense in our technology-driven world.

Dr. Martijn Dekker
Chief Information Security Officer ABN AMRO Bank

Chapter 1

The Imperative of Securing
Emerging Technologies

*"We live in a society exquisitely dependent on science and technology,
in which hardly anyone knows anything about science and technology."*
– Carl Sagan, Astronomer

For bonuses go to ...

1

The Rise of Emerging Technologies:
A Double-Edged Sword

*"Success in creating AI would be the biggest event
in human history. Unfortunately, it might also be the last,
unless we learn how to avoid the risks."*
– Stephen Hawking, Physicist

The pace of change has never been this fast, yet it will never be this slow again.

In 1996, two Stanford University graduate students, Larry Page and Sergey Brin, developed PageRank as part of a research project about a new kind of search engine. This innovation, born in the early days of the internet, reflects a key moment in digital history. It underscores how groundbreaking ideas often emerge from understanding and leveraging the foundational technologies of the time. PageRank was a groundbreaking way to rank websites by analyzing the number and quality of links to a website to estimate its importance and reliability. This innovative algorithm would form the foundation of Google, today's largest search engine, which Page and Brin launched in 1998. As of

January 2024, Google.com accounted for a whopping 84% of the global desktop internet search market. In the early 2000s, the internet and its accompanying search capabilities were themselves emerging technologies that would profoundly change our world.

But what exactly does the term "emerging technologies" entail? Essentially, emerging technologies are those that represent progressive, often disruptive developments within a field that offer a competitive advantage. They are in their infancy but promise profound change. Examples span a wide range, from artificial intelligence to quantum computing, robotics, cryptocurrencies, biotechnology, and many more, some of which we will cover in this book. Typically, these are technologies at the cutting edge of innovation, characterized by rapid growth, significant investment interest, and the potential to impact multiple sectors.

Emerging technologies may initially appear insignificant, making little to no noticeable impact. A prime example of this deceptive beginning is the mobile phone, which Motorola invented in 1973. The prototype was bulky, weighing 1.1 kg (2.4 lb.), offered a mere 30 minutes of talk time, required a 10-hour recharge, and was priced at $3,995, equivalent to approximately $10,000 today. However, the cellular revolution that began in the 90s popularized mobile phones. In 1990, the number of mobile users was around 11 million. Fast forward to 2024, and the number has skyrocketed to an astonishing 7.41 billion. This evolution was propelled by advancements in battery technology, miniaturization of electronic components, and the global expansion of cellular networks, marking a shift from bulky prototypes to the sleek smartphones of today.

When they succeed, emerging technologies transform how we live, work, communicate, and interact with the world around us. Take, for instance, the growing popularity of the Internet of Things (IoT) or "smart devices." British technologist Kevin Ashton coined the term IoT in 1999, to describe the network of physical objects embedded with sensors and software that allow them to connect to the internet and exchange data.

It is estimated that the number of IoT devices installed worldwide will reach 51 billion in 2023, with a staggering increase to 75 billion by 2025. To put these numbers in perspective, there were only an estimated 15 billion IoT devices in 2015. The exponential growth of these devices is impressive and worrisome, especially for cybersecurity professionals. Each device represents a potential point of entry for cybercriminals, and sadly, many IoT devices lack robust security measures. The rush to market, cost constraints, and a general lack of security awareness often result in these devices becoming easy targets for malicious activities like large-scale attacks, data breaches, and service disruptions.

A notorious example was the Mirai Botnet attack in 2016. The malware targeted IoT devices like cameras and routers, commandeering them into a network of remotely controlled "bots." These bots were then utilized by cybercriminals to launch a massive Distributed Denial of Service (DDoS) attack on Dyn's servers, a major Domain Name System (DNS) provider. This attack caused a temporary outage of major websites like Twitter, Netflix, Reddit, and Airbnb, among others, vividly illustrating the type of disruptions weak cybersecurity can cause. To prevent such attacks, it is essential to implement rigorous security protocols, which will be covered in more detail later in this book.

The Mirai Botnet attack underscores the complex dynamics of our relationship with emerging technologies. On one hand, these sophisticated technologies promise unprecedented levels of convenience, efficiency, and productivity. On the other hand, they introduce new vulnerabilities that malicious entities can exploit to cause significant harm. This is the double-edged sword of technological progress, a balance between the promise of technology and the potential risks it may present.

"It was the best of times, it was the worst of times, it was the age of wisdom, it was the age of foolishness, it was the epoch of belief, it was the epoch of incredulity, it was the season of Light, it was the season of Darkness, it was the spring of hope, it was the winter of despair, we had everything before us, we had nothing before us...."
– Charles Dickens, author of *A Tale of Two Cities*

As emerging technologies mature and proliferate, they often reveal new challenges and threats. While we can see and appreciate the potential of these technologies to improve our lives, we must also recognize the potential dangers and vulnerabilities they introduce.

Many of the emerging technologies explored in this book are either general-purpose technologies like quantum computing and artificial intelligence, or those with high potential risk, like robotics and autonomous vehicles. Given the scale, complexity, and potential impact of these technologies, we must take care to design and secure them effectively. The fast pace of development and adoption underscores the urgency for a proactive, robust, and adaptive approach to cybersecurity. Thus, the rise of emerging technologies is a story of progress but also a call to action to secure our collective digital futures.

The challenge for innovative leaders is not just about understanding and exploiting these technologies but also appreciating the threats they pose and preparing for them. The balance between progress and security will guide you in exploring the transformative emerging technologies of our time.

Securing the Future: The Importance of Cybersecurity in Emerging Technologies

"Cybersecurity is a shared responsibility, and it boils down to this: in cybersecurity, the more systems we secure, the more secure we all are."
– Jeh Johnson, former US Secretary of Homeland Security

We live in an era of unprecedented technological development and innovation, where significant emerging technologies converge, interact, and progress concurrently. The collaborative impact of these technologies significantly alters every aspect of life, including our work, communication, entertainment, and approaches to global challenges.

The driving force behind this technological revolution is the remarkable growth in computing power, aligning with Moore's Law. This law was based on observations by Gordon Moore, the co-founder of Intel. In 1965, Moore contributed to the 35th anniversary issue of *Electronics* magazine, with a prediction on the future of the semiconductor components industry over the next ten years. His response was a brief article entitled "Cramming More Components onto Integrated Circuits," in which he predicted that the number of transistors on a microchip would double every two years, leading to an exponential increase in processing capabilities.

This exponential increase in computing power supports further advancements and breakthroughs in other fields. Microprocessor architects report that semiconductor advancements have slowed industry-wide since around 2010, below the pace predicted by Moore's law. In April 2005, Gordon Moore stated that the projection cannot continue indefinitely: *"It can't continue forever. The nature of exponentials is that you push them out and eventually disaster happens."*

Forecasters, including Gordon Moore, expect that Moore's law will end by around 2025. Although Moore's Law will reach a physical limitation, some are optimistic about the continued progress in several areas, including new chip architectures, quantum computing, AI, and machine learning.

But this sheer increase in computing power is only half of the story. The other crucial half is the democratization of this power, making it more accessible and affordable to more people. This accessibility enables a broader range of individuals, organizations, and nations to innovate and adopt emerging technologies, further fueling the pace of innovation.

In this technological era, artificial intelligence assists in accelerated medication development, robotics and automation are further enhancing manufacturing processes, quantum computing promises to solve complex computing problems, blockchain technology is disrupting traditional finance and government systems, and biotechnology is reshaping health care and agriculture.

As societies and economies become increasingly dependent on increasingly sophisticated technologies, the importance of cybersecurity becomes crucial. Securing these advanced technologies is imperative. The reasons are not just the potential damage a cyberattack could inflict, but the wider implications for society, economy, and individual privacy.

At a societal level, computing technologies enable the seamless operation of critical infrastructure; for example, healthcare systems, traffic management systems, or water supply networks. A cybersecurity attack on critical infrastructure could lead to catastrophic outcomes.

Individual privacy is also at stake. The data generated and processed by emerging technologies is often personal and sensitive. In the wrong hands, this data could be exploited to disastrous effect, leading to identity theft, financial fraud, or even extortion.

Consider one of the most destructive cybersecurity attacks in history. The NotPetya cyberattack shocked the world not only with its destructive powers but also with the breadth and speed of its spread. The world had never seen such a sophisticated cyberattack. It began in Ukraine on the 27th of June 2017, and rapidly spread worldwide, causing more damage than any other ransomware in history. NotPetya encrypted files on infected systems and forced users to pay a ransom to decrypt them.

Unlike traditional ransomware, NotPetya did not have a payment mechanism. It was wiperware masked as standard ransomware. Instead, it destroyed the master boot record, making it impossible for victims to restart their computers. NotPetya destroyed Windows-based servers and computers within around an hour after the initial infection. NotPetya caused billions of dollars in damage, paralyzing companies and governments around the world. Employees were locked out of computers, and vital data was destroyed.

The NotPetya incident is a reminder of the potential consequences of weak cybersecurity, particularly as we become more reliant on emerging technologies. Therefore, a proactive and robust approach to cybersecurity is critical to ensuring the sustainable and secure growth of our society and economy.

Securing emerging technologies is complex and evolving. It requires innovative leaders, like you, in business, technology, and policy, to understand and prioritize cybersecurity.

Remember, the technology of the future is only as strong as the security that safeguards it.

Thinking Like a Futurist: An Essential Skill in the Modern Age

"A scientist in his laboratory is not a mere technician; he is also a child confronting natural phenomena that impress him as though they were fairy tales."
– Marie Curie, Scientist

The accelerating pace of the current modern age, with emerging technologies shaping the present environment, promises to bring about even more profound changes in the future. Given this, a critical question arises: How can you prepare for what is next? As an innovative leader, the answer partially resides within a mindset that you must cultivate, and that is thinking like a futurist.

But what exactly is a futurist? A futurist or forecaster is not a predictor of future events, despite what the name suggests, but a professional who extrapolates from current trends and insights to envisage potential future scenarios. This manner of thinking does not revolve around accurately predicting every detail of the future. It is about understanding probable, possible, and preferable outcomes and preparing for them. This ability to think through and anticipate various versions of the future is especially valuable when applied to emerging technologies and cybersecurity, as it will equip you with the ability to anticipate and mitigate many of the risks associated with these technologies.

Futurists employ a variety of methodologies to think about the future. For this section, we have picked one of the most accessible methodologies, namely the Futures Cone.

When you consider the future, many things could potentially happen from this moment in time. The further into the future you extend your mind, the more potential futures emerge. The Futures Cone considers this expanding range of potential futures as a set of nested cones, with each cone representing a different degree of future likelihood, as follows:

- Projected/probable (likely) futures are those most likely to occur based on the current path and trajectory. Relating to cybersecurity and emerging technology, we can forecast probable futures based on existing technology trends and current cybersecurity challenges.

- Possible (less likely) futures are those that encompass a broader scope, including outcomes that are feasible but less likely unless we deviate from our current path. This may include potential cybersecurity challenges that could arise with the adoption of emerging technologies or societal behaviors.

- Preferable (desired) futures are those we actively desire and strive for, regardless of their likelihood. In terms of cybersecurity of emerging technologies, this encompasses our collective vision of a digitally secure world that provides a goal to work towards.

- Preposterous (very unlikely) futures are those that are entirely unlikely, ridiculous, or impossible, and therefore not useful to consider.

Thinking like a futurist allows you to examine the current state of cybersecurity challenges to emerging technologies. It encourages you to visualize a secure digital future and to take strategic steps today towards making that future a reality. This model enables you to anticipate potential issues before they become unmanageable, preparing you for a variety of scenarios and helping to shape strategies that secure the present and the future. You can foster this mindset within your teams by encouraging continuous learning, promoting cross-disciplinary thinking, and engaging in scenario-planning exercises to explore various future possibilities.

Consider, for example, the rise of artificial intelligence (AI) technologies. As AI becomes more pervasive, a possible future is one where cybersecurity threats become increasingly automated and sophisticated. By adopting a futurist perspective today and identifying this as a possible future, we can start developing AI-driven cybersecurity solutions, implementing regulations around AI safety, and educating stakeholders about potential threats.

The application of the futurist perspective is useful for all innovative business leaders, policymakers, educators, and individuals, and especially for cybersecurity professionals as securing the powerful emerging technologies that we will cover in this book will be vital to human prosperity. As we become more interconnected and reliant on advanced technologies for critical infrastructure, medical services, and food production, amongst others, we have a collective responsibility to manifest and work towards a preferred future, which is a secure future.

Fostering this secure digital future goes beyond just technology. It encompasses creating secure software and systems, practicing responsible data handling, considering ethical challenges, and maintaining continuous education about digital threats. Every positive action contributes more resilience.

In the face of rapid technological change, 'thinking like a futurist' is no longer a skill reserved for a select few. It is an essential perspective for you as an innovative leader. As you encounter and work on emerging technologies, be mindful of the future; steer towards a secure and empowering digital future.

The Dilemmas of Technology

"Whenever you take a step forward,
you are bound to disturb something."
— Indira Gandhi, third prime minister of India

Every technological advancement, while primarily aimed at driving positive transformation, is inherently plagued by certain challenges. From obvious threats, such as cyberattacks, to the nuanced ethical dilemmas posed by social media, and artificial intelligence. Navigating these predicaments is crucial for anyone responsible for developing or deploying technologies.

As you engage in the development or deployment of advanced technologies, you will encounter a series of challenging dilemmas. How do you harness the power of technology without becoming a victim of its potential pitfalls?

The Innovator's Dilemma: This term, coined by Harvard Professor Clayton M. Christensen, depicts how established companies can lose market leadership by overlooking disruptive technologies.

Netflix, initially a DVD rental-by-mail service, successfully navigated this dilemma by transitioning to a streaming service and investing in its own content creation, like the series *House of Cards*. Similarly, Apple, under Steve Jobs, shifted focus from traditional personal computers to disruptive products like the iPod, iPhone, and iPad, fundamentally altering how we consume media and communicate.

The Technology Adoption Dilemma: Adopting new technology is a balancing act between risk and reward. Early adopters might gain a competitive edge but could also expose themselves to unidentified risks, security or otherwise. On the other hand, late adopters may miss out on strategic opportunities despite minimizing security risks.

Early crypto adopters who invested in or mined cryptocurrencies like Bitcoin, in its early stages, faced a novel and potentially lucrative opportunity. However, alongside the potential for significant financial gains, they also encountered substantial risks. Many early adopters lost their coins through hacks, as the security infrastructure around cryptocurrencies was still developing. Additionally, issues like losing physical wallets (hardware devices storing cryptocurrency keys) or forgetting passwords to digital wallets were not uncommon. These challenges highlight the dilemma of adopting emerging technology early. The advantage of being a frontrunner in a potentially transformative space comes with the risk of facing unforeseen challenges and threats.

On the other hand, if you had bought $100 USD on 9 February 2011, when Bitcoin reached parity with the US dollar, on 1 January 2024, when Bitcoin was valued at $42,691.10, you would have $4,269,110.

The Digital Divide Dilemma: This refers to the growing gap between those who have access to digital technology and those who do not. This divide can lead to an unequal distribution of security risks and protections.

Examples include the gender divide, where women are less likely to own a phone or access the internet; the social divide, where unequal internet access leads to social stratification; and the universal access divide, where individuals with disabilities face barriers to using technology. A Pew Research Center study highlighted that in the USA, among adults with household incomes below $30,000, significant percentages lack smartphones, broadband services, or traditional computers.

The Collingridge/Regulation Dilemma: Named after British scientist David Collingridge, this dilemma highlights the predicament of regulating emerging technologies effectively. In the early stages of a new technology, we often lack a comprehensive understanding of its implications. By the time we comprehend its impacts, regulating it becomes significantly more challenging.

Considering social media, in its early stage, negative impacts like the spread of misinformation and cyberbullying were underestimated. When these issues surfaced, social media was already deeply entrenched in our society, making regulation complex and controversial.

Blockchain technology exemplifies this dilemma, having developed and proliferated rapidly in the past decade, but our collective decisions about governing it have only just started to develop. The internet's evolution is another example. Initially, it was seen as a tool for democratizing information, but it has also been used to reduce democratic freedoms through misinformation and disinformation, posing new challenges that were not anticipated in its early development.

The Privacy versus Security Dilemma: The digital age presents a continuous tug of war between individual privacy and collective security. Encryption tools that shield us from cyber threats can also infringe on societal security. Think of the debate around contact-tracing apps during the COVID-19 pandemic. While they were instrumental in controlling the spread of the virus, they also raised concerns about potential invasions of personal privacy.

An example is the internet's early days, sometimes described as the "no-privacy wild west." Social media outlets, advertising companies, and government agencies gathered vast amounts of data, sometimes pushing the boundaries of legality. This unrestricted data collection presented significant privacy concerns, countered by the development of privacy-enhancing tools like encrypted messaging services. However, these tools create challenges for law enforcement, who cannot get access to these messages as easily. The more private the user data, the harder it is to monitor malicious activities.

The Security versus Usability Dilemma: This dilemma is a common predicament in software design. There is often a trade-off between enhancing security and maintaining user-friendly design. An overly secured system may not be user-friendly, while a system designed for ease of use may overlook crucial security aspects.

To turn these dilemmas into opportunities, you should cultivate a culture that values innovation while prioritizing safety and security. You should strive for an environment that encourages the exploration of new ideas and technologies while cultivating a deep understanding of their potential risks and implications. Understanding these technology dilemmas serves as a roadmap to anticipate potential roadblocks when adopting emerging technologies.

In this balancing act, regulation plays a pivotal role. We need flexible regulations that evolve in tandem with technological advancements. Policymakers should work closely with technologists, cybersecurity experts, and ethicists to design regulations that protect users and society without stifling innovation.

Democratization of Technology: Cybersecurity Implications

"The number one benefit of information technology is that it empowers people to do what they want to do."
– Steve Ballmer, former CEO of Microsoft

One of the wonderful characteristics of digital technologies is the tendency to become more affordable over time, making it accessible to more people, a sort of democratization of technology. Today, what was once the exclusive domain of academics, experts, and governments, is now readily accessible to many people. From smartphones to artificial intelligence, tools and platforms once considered science fiction are now commonplace.

This widespread access to technology is leveling the playing field, igniting innovation, and reshaping industries. At the same time comes the amplification of risks and potential negative outcomes, especially cybersecurity risks.

The spread of advanced emerging technologies to more individuals and organizations has dramatically increased the potential for cyberattacks.

Each smart device, software, and user represents a possible entry point for malicious actors, including more vulnerable members of society like your children or elderly parents.

In an interconnected world, a breach in one area can impact the entire digital landscape. In late 2020, the SolarWinds cyberattack unfolded, and it is a sobering example of such shockwaves. SolarWinds, a widely used provider of network management software, unwittingly became the source of one of the most extensive and audacious cyber espionage campaigns in recent history. A sophisticated attack on SolarWinds' software update process allowed threat actors to load a malicious backdoor into their software. As a result, countless organizations that relied on SolarWinds' products inadvertently installed the compromised updates.

Even without considering the SolarWinds example, consider the masses of data generated, used, and stored by advanced technologies, like artificial intelligence systems. As businesses and individuals come to rely more on data-driven insights, this information becomes increasingly valuable. Not only is there the risk of data exposure, but in the hands of cybercriminals, it can lead to identify theft, manipulation, or misuse of data, with consequences ranging from financial loss to reputational damage.

To address these heightened risks, cybersecurity awareness and improved controls must become universal. It should not remain the sole concern of IT departments or specialized firms. Everyone, from individual users to large corporations, from educators to students, must possess a foundational understanding of cybersecurity.

This starts with adopting elementary precautions such as deploying strong, unique passwords, embracing two-factor authentication, and ensuring timely software updates. More advanced measures, like recognizing phishing threats, adjusting data privacy settings, and understanding the rudiments of secure networks, should also be part of the common discourse.

The widespread availability of powerful computing devices has enabled both unprecedented access to information and an increase in the scale and sophistication of cyberattacks, highlighting the need for universal cybersecurity literacy. For this reason, incorporating cybersecurity education at schools, homes, and within workplaces is imperative. When people become technologically savvy, they should concurrently become adept at safeguarding their digital lives.

The democratization of technology, while transformative, ushers in a novel set of cybersecurity challenges. But by embracing these challenges and addressing them proactively, you can harness the full potential of democratized technology. As an innovative leader, you are one of the pioneers of our future, and collectively, we must protect it.

A Call to Action for Cybersecurity in Emerging Technologies

"The advance of technology is based on making it fit in so that you don't really even notice it, so it's part of everyday life."
— Bill Gates, founder of Microsoft

We stand at a pivotal moment. The allure and potential of emerging technologies are undeniable; their capacity to transform our world is immense. However, as we have explored in this chapter, emerging technologies bring with them a host of new challenges and risks. This dual nature of emerging technologies underscores an urgent and essential call to action. We must insist upon and develop a secure digital future.

This is not a responsibility to be shouldered by a select few. It is a collective effort that involves all of us. Whether you are a technology professional, a business leader, a policymaker, an educator, or an individual consumer, you have a vital role to play.

- **Technology professionals and business leaders:** Emphasize "security by design." Make every digital product secure. Champion this culture within your organizations.

- **Policymakers:** Draft regulations that are as dynamic as the technology landscape. Collaborate cross-discipline to ensure rules protect without impeding progress.

- **Educators:** Forge the next generation of digital citizens. Integrate cybersecurity into curriculums, ensuring awareness from the earliest stages.

- **Individual consumer:** Buy products that have been securely developed by reputable vendors. Your digital habits shape our collective security. Practice robust cybersecurity and share this knowledge within your community.

As you journey through this book, do not just passively consume the information. Use it to empower yourself and make a positive difference in your respective spheres. Collective positive actions can shape the future of society and the use of emerging technologies, steering them towards a path that maximizes their potential while mitigating their risks. The imperative of securing emerging technologies is indeed a call to action, a call to you to step up, take responsibility, and contribute to building a secure, resilient, and empowering digital future. The quest to secure emerging technologies is not just a challenge; it is an invitation. How will you respond?

Chapter 2

Future-Proofing Cybersecurity: The Next Generation of Computing

"Digital technology, pervasively, is getting embedded in every place: everything, every person, every walk of life is being fundamentally shaped by digital technology—it is happening in our homes, our work, our places of entertainment. It's amazing to think of a world as a computer. I think that's the right metaphor for us as we go forward."
– Satya Nadella, CEO of Microsoft

For bonuses go to ...

The Cybersecurity Implications
of Evolving Computing

"The only thing that is constant is change."
— Heraclitus, Greek philosopher

The rise and fall of Blockbuster, once a titan in the home movie and video game rental industry, offers a compelling lesson in the necessity of adaptation in the face of technological evolution. Founded in 1985, Blockbuster dominated the American market until the late 1990s. The advent of DVDs and the emergence of Netflix, an online DVD rental service established in 1997, signaled a seismic shift in the industry. Unfortunately, Blockbuster failed to adapt to a rapidly changing world, where streaming services and digital downloads were quickly rendering physical rentals obsolete. On September 23, 2010, the organization filed for Chapter 11 bankruptcy protection. The final organization-owned Blockbuster store shut its doors in 2014.

Imagine the vast, well-lit aisles of a Blockbuster store in the 1990s, stacked with VHS tapes and later DVDs. Now, contrast that image with today's streaming services, where thousands of movies and TV shows can be accessed with a few clicks or taps on a screen. This transformation is

24

nothing short of remarkable. But it also illustrates a broader point, which is that every leap in technological capabilities and every shift in how technology is deployed and consumed, brings about a unique set of societal changes and consequently security challenges.

Blockbuster's decline was not just about failing to see the future of faster internet speeds and digital streaming. It was about failing to understand the massive shift that the internet and digital technologies represented. This shift not only redefined entertainment but also the entire landscape of cybersecurity. As Blockbuster clung to its business model based on physical stores, Netflix was adopting digital technologies. This adoption highlights the need for cybersecurity to evolve in tandem with technological advancements, ensuring that new digital platforms are not just innovative but also secure.

In today's world, where cyber threats can come from anywhere in the world and target any connected device, the lesson is simple and clear: Adapt or die. Of course, striking the right balance between embracing innovation and ensuring security is essential.

The story of Blockbuster serves as a parable for the broader world of cybersecurity. As technologies evolve, companies and institutions find themselves in a quandary. On one side, a mass of vulnerabilities awaits those who rush headlong into the latest technology without proper cybersecurity safeguards. On the other side, the threat of obsolescence waits for those who are too cautious and/or innovate too slowly.

To strike this balance, two key strategies emerge. First, organizations must embed security and privacy controls as integral components of product design, not as afterthoughts or burdensome overheads. Second, adaptive learning and a robust feedback loop are critical. Organizations should not only identify but also promptly address vulnerabilities, ensuring continuous improvement in their products and services.

While the book focusses much attention on cybersecurity, the significant challenges introduced by a rapidly developing legal and ethical landscape are acknowledged. This forces organizations to continuously adapt not only their security measures but also their data and privacy policies.

5G and Edge Computing: Redefining Network Security

"5G is not just faster internet; it's a paradigm shift."
– Unknown

The journey from the individual computers of the 1950s, to today's cloud-centric models, exemplifies a transformative leap in technology. We have witnessed the evolution from mainframe-based computing in the 1970s, client-server computing in the 1980s, to the internet-based and cloud computing technologies of today. Each phase has reshaped our approach to data processing and cybersecurity.

Today's computing landscape, dominated by massive data volumes and real-time processing, favors centralized cloud architectures. Giants like Amazon Web Solutions, Microsoft Azure, and Google Cloud have revolutionized scalability and accessibility. Yet, this centralization brings challenges, including latency, data sovereignty issues, potential failure points, and attracts cybercriminals.

Enter 5G and edge computing. These technologies facilitate high-speed processing closer to data sources, in technologies like IoT devices and autonomous vehicles, marrying distributed and cloud model strengths. This synergy aims to diminish latency, bolster data privacy, and secure ecosystem resilience.

- **5G: Beyond Speed:** The fifth generation (5G) mobile network transcends its predecessors (3G, 4G) in speed, reliability, and connectivity. Imagine the progression from a horse trail (1G) to a gravel road (2G), to a paved road (3G), to a highway (4G). 5G is like a hyperloop in data transport terms. The development of 5G sets the stage for even more advanced networks like 6G, promising further industry upheaval.

- **Edge Computing: Localized Efficiency:** This distributed computing paradigm brings data processing and storage closer to its source, minimizing latency and bandwidth consumption. It is a strategic optimization of cloud systems, enhancing data processing efficiency at the data source, be it an IoT device or a smartphone.

5G and Edge Computing in Action

While 5G and edge computing are two distinct technologies, together these technologies unlock groundbreaking applications, including:

- **Smart Cities:** Managing traffic, energy consumption, and public safety through real-time edge data analysis.

- **Autonomous Vehicles:** Enhancing safety and decision-making through local data processing and rapid vehicle-to-infrastructure communication.

- **AR and VR:** Delivering immersive experiences with minimal lag through rapid, localized data processing.

- **Health Care:** Facilitating remote surgeries and quick patient data processing at hospitals.

- **Agriculture:** Implementing precision farming with immediate data processing on soil and crop conditions.

- **Retail:** Offering personalized shopping experiences through instant data processing in smart mirrors.

These examples underscore the transformative potential of 5G and edge computing across various sectors. As these technologies continue to mature, we can expect more revolutionary applications to emerge. As we embrace these advancements, the necessity for integrated cybersecurity measures becomes more pronounced, ensuring these new technologies do not become liabilities.

It is important to consider the following cybersecurity challenges:

- **Multiple Access Points:** Billions of interconnected IoT devices present numerous entry points for cyberattacks. Unlike the fortified data centers of cloud service providers, IoT devices generally lack robust built-in security.

- **Increased Complexity:** The intricate nature of distributed architectures in edge computing complicates traditional network security, making the concept of a "security perimeter" obsolete.

- **Data Privacy:** Local processing increases data exposure risks, especially when data is processed on poorly secured devices.

- **Supply Chain Risks:** The global sourcing of 5G components introduces geopolitical cybersecurity risks.

- **Network Slicing:** The segmentation of 5G networks can escalate the scope of an attack if one segment is compromised.

- **Standardization:** The lack of uniform standards in decentralized networks poses significant security challenges.

To secure the future, where 5G and edge computing proliferate, addressing these vulnerabilities requires a multifaceted approach:

- **AI and Analytics:** Utilizing AI for real-time threat detection.

- **Zero-Trust Architecture:** Verifying all connections to the network.

- **Blockchain:** A powerful tool to ensure data integrity across the network.

- **Global Cooperation:** Developing frameworks and regulations that address unique security challenges in a unified manner.

- **Best Practices:** Implementing multi-factor authentication (MFA) and end-to-end encryption as standard security measures.

With this new computing paradigm, the combination of 5G and edge computing opens many possibilities and challenges. The key is to embrace these innovations while strengthening cybersecurity strategies, ensuring a safe and efficient integration into our digital future.

Brain-Computer Interfaces (BCIs): Protecting Brain-Inspired Tech

"We can only see a short distance ahead,
but we can see plenty there that needs to be done."
– Alan Turing, Computer Scientist, Cryptographer

In 2021, Neuralink, an organization founded by Elon Musk, released a video showing a macaque monkey named Pager, playing the video game Pong, using its mind. The monkey's brain signals were sent wirelessly via an implanted device.

Initially, Pager was taught to play the game with a joystick while enjoying a fruit smoothie as a reward. During this process, the Neuralink device recorded information about which neurons were firing to control which movements. The joystick was then disconnected, leaving Pager to control the game with his mind.

Historically, computers have existed as separate entities from their users. However, the emergence of brain-computer interfaces (BCIs) represents a new form of computing, where neurology and computer science converge. This convergence has the power to redefine our interactions with technology and with one another. They bridge the gap between human thoughts and digital devices, allowing for direct communication between a brain and an external device.

Brain-Computer Interfaces (BCIs): Protecting Brain-Inspired Tech

The evolution from individual computers to cloud-centric models heralded a revolution in computing. Similarly, the transition from traditional input mechanisms like keyboards and mice to direct BCIs is set to transform our interaction with technology. BCIs, also known as neural interfaces or brain-machine interfaces, create direct communication pathways between the brain and an external device. While this development is exciting, it introduces complex cybersecurity challenges that we must navigate.

Understanding BCIs and Their Potential

BCIs work by translating the brain's electrical activity into actionable commands for machines. This translation occurs through sensors placed on the scalp or, in advanced scenarios, directly implanted within the brain. These interfaces decode neural signals into specific commands, enabling actions like typing a document or controlling a drone, using only thought. In the medical field, BCIs show tremendous promise. For example, they could enable mobility for patients with paralysis through thought-controlled prosthetics and exoskeletons. In November 2022, the University of Texas demonstrated a mind-controlled wheelchair, offering new mobility avenues for paralyzed individuals by translating users' thoughts into mechanical commands.

Applications Beyond Medicine

Beyond medical applications, BCIs have the potential to revolutionize augmented reality (AR) and virtual reality (VR), providing immersive experiences controlled by the user's thoughts. In educational settings, BCIs could tailor learning experiences by monitoring a student's concentration and brain activity. Additionally, for individuals unable to speak, BCIs have already shown promise in converting thoughts into text or speech, as evidenced by the achievements of researchers from Radboud University and UMC Utrecht in August 2023.

Cybersecurity Risks in BCIs

The intimate connection between BCIs and their users introduces unprecedented cybersecurity challenges, where a breach could have deeply personal consequences. The unique cybersecurity challenges of BCIs cannot be overstated. Hacking BCIs equates to hacking human thoughts, presenting risks previously unseen in technology. These risks include:

- **Mind Hacking:** The interception and manipulation of neural data could lead to unprecedented privacy violations, as it involves accessing and potentially altering thoughts.

- **Device Tampering:** Like vulnerabilities in computing devices, BCI hardware could be susceptible to unauthorized access, leading to false data interpretation or physical harm.

- **Data Integrity:** The authenticity and security of data from BCIs are critical, especially in medical applications where tampered data could result in incorrect diagnoses or device malfunctions.

- **Legal and Ethical Implications:** The ability to access and influence a user's thoughts or memories raises significant ethical questions. Issues of cognitive liberty, neural data ownership, and individual rights require careful consideration and the development of robust legal frameworks.

Just as with other emerging technologies, a proactive approach to cybersecurity is vital as BCIs become more integrated into society. Some strategies include:

- **End-to-End Encryption:** To protect privacy, encrypting data transmitted between the brain and devices is crucial.

- **Robust Authentication:** Given the sensitivity of BCI data, implementing strong authentication and biometric checks is vital; these include, amongst others, cognitive biometrics and electroencephalography (EEG).

- **AI and Machine Learning:** Employing these technologies to detect anomalies in neural data can help identify potential threats in real time.

- **Ethical Frameworks:** Collaboration between technology developers, governments, and ethicists is necessary to establish guidelines and regulations for user protection. For example, the US

Food and Drug Administration (FDA) issued guidance on "Implanted Brain-Computer Interface (BCI) Devices for Patients with Paralysis or Amputation – Non-clinical Testing and Clinical Considerations," in May 2021. The IEEE has standards for "Neurotechnologies for Brain-Machine Interfacing."

The world of BCIs is a testament to the limitless bounds of human imagination, innovation, and technological progress. As the merging of mind and machine progresses, we must tread carefully, ensuring that the desire for progress does not overshadow the need for safety and ethics. There are calls for human rights protections on emerging brain-computer interfaces. In this new era, it is not just your devices but your mind and thoughts that must be safeguarded.

Spatial Computing: A New Dimension in Computing and Cybersecurity

"It's tomorrow's engineering, today."
–Tim Cook, CEO Apple Inc., presenting the Apple Vision Pro

Personal computing has evolved from clunky desktop computers to sleek laptops, and subsequently to more portable form factors like smart phones and tablets. When we present at conferences and ask the audience who is carrying a smart phone, this elicits a laugh, and every hand is raised. Some carry two or more mobile or connected devices. Considering that the first Apple iPhone was released in 2007, within a span of just over a decade, smart phones have become ubiquitous and are now an integral part of our daily lives.

We are experiencing another radical shift in computing. The journey from desktops to smartphones has been remarkable. With the advent of Apple Vision Pro and other spatial computing devices, we are entering an era where our digital and physical worlds converge. This transformative development marks a profound change in how we engage with technology, blurring the boundaries between the virtual and the real.

At its core, spatial computing is an advanced blend of augmented reality (AR) and virtual reality (VR). Unlike AR, which overlays digital elements onto the real world, or VR, which immerses you in a digital environment, spatial computing is essentially a mix of these two. This technology relies on sophisticated sensors, 3D rendering, and machine learning algorithms to create an interactive space where physical and digital objects coexist and interact seamlessly.

Cybersecurity at the Forefront

Addressing the cybersecurity challenges of spatial computing requires a cross-disciplinary approach, blending expertise in digital security, physical safety, and user privacy. It is no surprise that the integration of digital and physical worlds brings unique cybersecurity challenges. In this space, the most obvious one is environmental hacking. Environmental hacking leads to the manipulation of augmented reality layers, causing misinformation or physical harm. This is a new attack vector that this innovative technology introduces.

A notable example is the modification of AR navigation systems, where hackers could potentially redirect users to unsafe locations or create hazardous distractions. In July 2016, Pokémon Go was launched by Niantic, a San Francisco-based game developer. Pokémon Go was one of the first games to successfully implement AR on a large scale. This allowed players to see Pokémon characters in their real-world surroundings through their phone screens, creating an immersive gaming experience. Some of the unintended consequences from the game included user injuries from potholes, lampposts, and collisions with other obstacles. A study from Purdue University's Krannert School of Management reported a disproportionate increase in vehicle crashes, personal injuries, and fatalities in the vicinity of locations, called PokéStops, where users could play the game while driving.

Similarly, in virtual reality (VR) scenarios, hackers can exploit system vulnerabilities to manipulate users' perceptions or steal sensitive data through seemingly innocuous virtual interactions. As spatial computing technologies advance and find broader applications, from health care to urban planning, the implications of such environment hacking become increasingly significant.

However, environmental hacking is not the only cybersecurity risk to worry about. Some of the cybersecurity challenges emerging with this technology are:

- **Data Privacy and Confidentiality:** As spatial computing often involves the collection and processing of personal data, including detailed views of your surroundings, it is crucial to ensure that this data is handled securely and confidentially. This includes implementing strong encryption methods and ensuring compliance with data protection regulations.

- **Secure Network Communications:** The data transmitted between devices in a spatial computing environment should be secured to prevent interception or manipulation. This could involve the use of secure communication protocols and encryption.

- **Device Integrity:** Devices used in spatial computing should be designed to resist tampering or hacking. This could include secure boot mechanisms, hardware-based security features, and regular software updates to address any identified vulnerabilities.

- **Sensor Vulnerabilities:** Spatial computing relies heavily on sensors to detect and interpret the environment. Any vulnerabilities in these sensors can be exploited to feed false information or even spy on users.

- **Interference with Other Systems:** Given the immersive nature of spatial computing, there is potential for interference with other critical systems, especially in sectors like aviation, health care, or transportation.

In this space, user education and awareness is paramount. Users should be made aware of the potential security risks associated with spatial computing, and provided with guidance on how to use these technologies safely. This could include training on recognizing and avoiding phishing attempts, setting strong passwords, and understanding privacy settings.

Spatial computing brings forward a future where the line between digital and physical blurs. The exciting opportunities it brings are matched by the cybersecurity challenges it presents. As with all technological revolutions, a proactive, collaborative approach to security will be the key to safely navigating this new dimension of computing. After all, in the era of spatial computing, it is not just our devices but our very environments that need protection.

Quantum Computing: The Quantum Leap in Cybersecurity and Cyberthreats

"A classical computation is like a solo voice—one line of pure tones succeeding each other. A quantum computation is like a symphony— many lines of tones interfering with one another."
– Seth Lloyd, professor of mechanical engineering and physics at the Massachusetts Institute of Technology (MIT)

In the world of quantum physics, intuition and common sense take a back seat. Particles can be in multiple states simultaneously, called superposition, and can be weirdly connected regardless of distance, called entanglement. These seemingly bizarre phenomena are not just curious observations; they are the driving forces behind quantum computing, which promises computational feats deemed impossible by classical computing.

Before we get you excited, let us back up just a bit and cover some basic definitions. Classical computers, the ones we all know and use today, are based on a binary system where bits can only exist as a 0 or a 1, which while very powerful, has some limitations. Quantum computers, by contrast, use quantum bits or qubits that can exist as a superposition of these two states and are able to process vast amounts of data at once. This means quantum computers have an immense potential for exponential growth in computing power compared to their classical counterparts. Think of it like turning on a switch that, instead of being just on or off, can be in a mysterious blend of both.

Quantum computing is the answer to problems deemed insurmountable for classical computers. Tasks that would take millennia for today's supercomputers, could potentially be solved in minutes by a sufficiently advanced quantum computer. Imagine a vault with billions of combinations. A classical computer would attempt to unlock it by trying each combination, one by one. A quantum computer, however, in its uncanny style, might explore multiple combinations at once.

Breakthroughs in fields like cryptography, material science, medicine, and even financial modeling are within reach. In 2022, a team at the California Institute of Technology used a quantum algorithm to simulate a complex molecule's behavior. This was previously considered intractable for classical machines.

Global investment in quantum computing has been substantial. In 2021, venture capitalists invested more than US$1 billion into the sector. By 2022, investors poured $2.35 billion into quantum technology start-ups. National governments have also significantly contributed, investing billions into quantum computing research.

As part of its five-year plan for quantum technology, 2021–2025, China has announced the most public funding to date of any country, more than double the investments by EU governments and eight times more than US government investments.

These investments reflect the growing recognition of the potential of quantum computing across various industries, including automotive, chemicals, financial services, and life sciences. Quantum technology is rapidly advancing toward commercial viability, representing one of the most significant technology arms races of our lives. The country that develops and deploys quantum computing first, is likely to have a significant competitive advantage, with major implications for geopolitics.

Even though quantum computers are still being developed, researchers are already working to protect sensitive data from the expected attacks resulting in advances in computing power. In anticipation, in August 2023, Google announced the release of code for a security key that uses cryptography designed to withstand decryption attempts by traditional computers and quantum processors as well. But while quantum computing attacks are still hypothetical, Google says that "deploying cryptography at internet scale is a massive undertaking," so it is important to get started as soon as possible. If you develop a product that is future-proof, it is likely to have more traction and success than a competitor who appears to be using old technology and does not appear to be proactive with their security practices.

The promise of quantum computing is not without pitfalls, especially when it comes to cybersecurity. Ironically, the same immense power that quantum computers wield can also undermine the very security protocols we rely upon today.

The vulnerabilities posed by quantum computing are diverse and multi-layered:

- **Decryption Abilities:** Traditional encryption methods, the backbone of modern cybersecurity, could be decrypted with ease by powerful quantum machines. Current encryption algorithms, which could take billions of years for classical computers to crack, might fall in mere hours or even minutes using quantum computers.

- **Quantum Eavesdropping:** In quantum communications, any attempt to eavesdrop changes the quantum state of the information being intercepted, making eavesdropping detectable. But as quantum technologies evolve, sophisticated methods to intercept without detection may emerge.

- **Software Vulnerabilities:** Quantum software is still in its nascent stages. As with any new technology, vulnerabilities may be discovered, offering cybercriminals new attack vectors.

- **Physical Security:** Quantum computers need extremely controlled environments, like intense cold (close to absolute zero). Any disturbances can affect qubit behavior, so physical attacks, like tampering with the cooling mechanism, could disrupt quantum operations.

While the threats are real, so are the countermeasures. While quantum computing presents formidable challenges to current cybersecurity models, it simultaneously opens doors to radically new forms of secure communication and encryption:

- **Post-Quantum Cryptography:** Anticipating the quantum threat, researchers are developing new cryptographic algorithms that remain resilient even in the face of quantum decryption capabilities. The algorithms and protocols they build are called quantum-resistant algorithms.

- **Quantum Key Distribution:** By transmitting information about the key in a quantum state, any interception attempt can be detected, making the key distribution process ultra-secure. The downside is that the beginning and end points of this communication must be two physical points in the world, which is an architecture that rarely exists in a virtual and cloudy world.

While powerful quantum computers are still in development and largely theoretical, the possibilities are endless and exciting. As we harness the power of quantum computing, we must ensure a commitment to safety; because, in this era, not just classical but also quantum security must be meticulously implemented.

Chapter 3

Artificial Intelligence and Machine Learning: Power, Pitfalls, and Protection

"If a machine is expected to be infallible, it cannot also be intelligent."
– Alan Turing, pioneer in the field of
computer science and artificial intelligence

3

AI and ML Systems: Power and Pitfalls

"The development of AI is as fundamental as the creation of
the microprocessor, the personal computer, the internet, and the mobile phone.
It will change the way people work, learn, travel, get health care, and communicate
with each other. Entire industries will reorient around it.
Businesses will distinguish themselves by how well they use it."
— Bill Gates, co-founder of Microsoft

In March 2016, a significant milestone in the field of artificial intelligence (AI) occurred when AlphaGo, an AI program created by DeepMind, a part of Alphabet Inc., defeated Lee Sedol, one of the world's top players, in the ancient board game of Go.

The game, Go, known for its strategic depth, had been a game where AI struggled to match human proficiency. This was due to the immense number of possible moves and the game's reliance on deep, intuitive thinking. AlphaGo's approach, using a combination of deep neural networks and reinforcement learning, was groundbreaking. It learned from large datasets of professional games, and improved by playing countless simulations against itself.

The match, held in Seoul, South Korea, was a best-of-five contest. It attracted global attention as AlphaGo demonstrated not just raw computing power but also a level of creativity and strategic understanding that was previously thought to be unique to humans. AlphaGo won four of the five games, showcasing an unprecedented level of AI capability in one of the most complex board games.

This event was more than a remarkable achievement in a game; it was a profound demonstration of the advances in AI. AlphaGo's victory illustrated that AI could handle tasks requiring not just calculation but also a form of creativity and intuition. The defeat of Lee Sedol by AlphaGo was a pivotal moment, reshaping our understanding of AI's potential and setting the stage for future developments in the field. Artificial intelligence (AI) and machine learning (ML) have emerged as transformative technologies, revolutionized various industries, and reshaped the way we interact with technology.

But before we go too far, let us get some definitions out of the way.

Artificial intelligence (AI) refers to the simulation of human intelligence in machines that are programmed to think and learn like humans. For example, an AI system can be programmed to diagnose diseases by analyzing medical images, mimicking the diagnostic process of a human doctor.

Machine learning, a subset of AI, takes this a step further by empowering systems to automatically learn and improve from experience without being explicitly programmed. A notable instance of ML is a recommendation algorithm used by streaming services, which learns viewers' preferences over time to suggest personalized content.

The origins of AI trace back to the mid-20th century, with seminal works like Turing's concept of a "universal machine" and the Dartmouth workshop in 1956, often considered the birth of AI as a field. Over the decades, AI evolved from simple rule-based systems to sophisticated machine learning algorithms capable of learning from data. The 21st century saw a renaissance in AI, fueled by the availability of big data, increased computational power, and advancements in algorithms, particularly in deep learning.

AI and ML are remarkable because, unlike traditional computer programs that follow pre-defined instructions, AI and ML models are capable of learning and adapting over time. They analyze incoming data, draw patterns, make predictions, and refine their predictions based on feedback. This dynamic nature allows them to improve their performance with every interaction. For instance, a chatbot learns from each conversation it has, progressively enhancing its ability to understand and respond to user requests. Similarly, a self-driving car uses real-time data from sensors to continuously improve its driving strategy. By harnessing the power of AI and ML, we can build more effective, adaptable, and intelligent systems that improve over time, unlocking unprecedented potential for progress across various fields.

AI has found widespread applications across various industries, transforming the way we work and live. In health care, AI aids in medical diagnosis, drug development, and personalized treatment plans. Financial institutions use AI for fraud detection, risk assessment, and algorithmic trading. AI-powered virtual assistants enhance customer experiences in the retail and service sectors. Additionally, AI is pivotal in optimizing supply chains, predicting maintenance needs in manufacturing, and improving agriculture practices.

Generative AI

Generative AI, an advanced use of AI, effectively reignited the interest in AI, with its capacity to create new content, be it text, images, music, or video. The most popular form of generative AI models is the large language model (LLM). The catalyst for the current AI wave was the introduction of ChatGPT by OpenAI in Nov 2022. ChatGPT leverages generative AI to produce human-like text based on received input.

ChatGPT's ability to generate human-like text responses has found applications in customer service, content creation, and education, amongst others. ChatGPT's success has highlighted the societal and technological impacts of generative AI, including ethical considerations like potential misuse and the influence on job markets. Its adoption illustrates the growing comfort and reliance of society on AI technologies for diverse applications.

Not to be outdone by OpenAI, other major technology organizations rapidly released various generative AI language models of their own:

- **Bing by Microsoft:** Bing's AI capabilities utilize ChatGPT.

- **Gemini by Google:** Introduced in December 2023, Gemini was touted as Google's most capable AI model, capable of understanding and responding to not only text but also code, audio, images, and video. This capability is commonly referred to as multimodal.

- **Llama 2 by Meta:** Llama 2 launched in July 2023, and was introduced by Meta as an open-source LLM, making it free for research and commercial use.

- **Claude by Anthropic:** Claude, launched in March 2023, is an LLM that can generate text, write code, and function as an AI assistant like ChatGPT.

Generative AI is disruptive primarily due to its ability to create new, original content. This feature sets it apart from other AI systems that are primarily decision-based or reactive. With generative AI, systems are no longer bound by the data they have been fed. They can write, compose, and design in a way that was previously thought to be uniquely human.

This technology is transforming industries where content creation is pivotal. In entertainment, generative AI can write scripts, compose music, and create virtual performers. In design, it can generate new concepts for products, architecture, and fashion. In journalism, it can draft articles based on provided data. It is also revolutionizing customer service, as AI can now generate personalized responses rather than selecting from pre-written scripts.

The year following the launch of ChatGPT saw an impressive acceleration in development and enhancements. Thanks to continuous learning from vast amounts of text data and iterative feedback from millions of users, the system's ability to generate coherent, relevant, and even creative responses improved significantly. One of the most significant advancements was the improvement in its contextual understanding, enabling the model to generate responses that are more aligned with the nuances of the conversation.

However, as with any AI system, it is important to be cognizant of the ethical implications and potential misuse. In response to this, OpenAI has made significant strides in implementing use-case policy and moderation tools to mitigate misuse while continuously refining the system based on user feedback and societal input. The journey of ChatGPT represents the rapid pace at which AI is progressing, underscoring the importance of robust AI governance and the potential of generative AI as a powerful tool for the future.

Data privacy is another pressing concern. As users interact with AI systems, they often feed the system confidential or sensitive information. Without stringent data privacy measures and policies, there is a risk of this information being exposed or misused. AI systems learn and improve based on the data they process; hence, the data must be anonymized and securely stored to prevent unauthorized access. It is also crucial to ensure that the AI does not inadvertently reveal sensitive information in its generated responses. This emphasizes the need for robust data privacy guidelines and regulations, alongside advanced security technologies, to safeguard user data and prevent misuse.

Safeguarding the Sources:
Protecting Training Data in AI and ML

"The more they track us and engage us, the more data they gather,
the better they can target, manipulate, and predict future behavior—
insights that they sell to lucrative markets of business customers."
– Shoshana Zuboff, author of *The Age of Surveillance Capitalism*

In 2016, Uber, the ride-hailing organization, was embroiled in a major data breach that affected the personal information of over 57 million drivers and passengers. The breach, which was discovered months after it occurred, was attributed to a flaw in the organization's software, which allowed hackers to obtain access to user data stored on its servers.

The occurrence underscores the potential exposure of large quantities of data to cybersecurity incidents. Uber's AI-powered algorithms rely heavily on the personal data of its users to provide efficient and personalized services. However, the breach exposed the inherent risks of storing such sensitive data on centralized servers, making it vulnerable to cyberattacks.

The core challenge in securing AI and ML systems lies in preserving the integrity, confidentiality, and availability of training data. This task extends beyond traditional data security, which focuses on data at rest and in transit. AI and ML systems depend heavily on their training data, which directly influences the system's learning, predictive capabilities, and output. This data often encompasses a diverse array of information including text, images, audio, and structured data.

Here are some of the differences between AI data security and traditional data security, each with unique characteristics and approaches.

- **Adversarial Attacks:** AI and ML systems can be vulnerable to adversarial attacks, where malicious actors deliberately manipulate input data to deceive or confuse the system. These attacks exploit the system's vulnerabilities and can lead to incorrect decisions. Protecting against such attacks requires understanding potential weaknesses and implementing countermeasures that bolster the system's resilience.

- **Data Leakage:** Unlike traditional systems, AI and ML models can inadvertently reveal sensitive information present in their training data. This phenomenon, known as data leakage, occurs when the model learns to replicate patterns present in the training data that might be personally identifiable or sensitive. Potential safeguards involve careful preprocessing of the training data to remove such information before training.

- **Model Inversion Attacks:** Attackers can reverse-engineer AI models to infer sensitive training data from the model's outputs. This is particularly concerning in cases where the model has been trained on private or confidential data. Robust security measures must consider these privacy concerns and implement techniques such as differential privacy to mitigate risks.

Differential privacy (DP) is a framework for ensuring the privacy of individuals in datasets. It provides a way to analyze data without revealing sensitive information about any individual in the dataset, achieved by making small changes to individual data that do not significantly alter the statistics of interest.

Next, let us explore strategies for safeguarding AI systems from training data attacks.

- **Data Augmentation:** Introducing synthetic variations into the training data can help the model become more resistant to adversarial attacks. By exposing the model to a wider range of inputs, it learns to generalize better and becomes less susceptible to manipulation.

- **Adversarial Training:** Incorporating adversarial examples into the training process can enhance the model's ability to recognize and reject manipulated inputs. This involves training the model with both legitimate and adversarial data to improve its robustness.

- **Regular Model Updates:** Keeping AI and ML models up to date is crucial for security. Regular updates help mitigate vulnerabilities that may emerge over time and ensure that the model remains effective against evolving threats.

- **Explainable AI (XAI):** Implementing XAI techniques can enhance the transparency of AI systems, making it easier to identify potential vulnerabilities and malicious inputs. Interpretable models allow security experts to understand how the system arrives at its decisions, aiding in the detection of anomalous behavior.

- **Federated Learning:** This approach enables training AI models across multiple devices or servers while keeping the training data localized. This minimizes the risk of exposing sensitive data during the training process and provides an added layer of security.

- **Secure Aggregation:** In scenarios where federated learning isn't feasible, secure aggregation techniques can be employed to protect the privacy of training data during the aggregation process.

- **Data Anonymization and Masking:** Before sharing training data with third parties or using it for collaborative projects, anonymizing and masking techniques can be employed to ensure that sensitive information is derisked.

Safeguarding training data in AI and ML systems requires a paradigm shift from traditional data security approaches. The unique challenges posed by adversarial attacks, data leakage, and model inversion require specialized measures to ensure the integrity and privacy of training data.

Data Poisoning: Corrupting the Learning Process

"The corruption of the best things gives rise to the worst."
– David Hume, Scottish philosopher

The AI revolution is powered by data, the digital gold that powers the machine-learning algorithms. Adversaries keenly understand that the quality of this data directly influences the efficacy of AI models. Data poisoning is a stealthy and subversive technique that involves injecting tainted or malicious data into the training dataset, with the aim of corrupting the learning process. These seemingly innocent outliers or subtle manipulations skew the AI model's understanding, causing it to produce inaccurate or even detrimental outcomes.

A well-known example of an adversarial attack on an AI system through data poisoning is Microsoft's Twitter chatbot, Tay. Released in 2016, Tay was designed to be a friendly bot interacting with Twitter users. However, malicious actors fed Tay a series of harmful and vulgar tweets, which drastically altered the output. This led to Tay responding in inappropriate and offensive ways, forcing Microsoft to withdraw the chatbot from the platform.

Imagine a financial institution utilizing AI to make lending decisions. Now, imagine attackers tampering with the training data by introducing a series of fraudulent loan applications. The AI model, as a result, learns distorted patterns and erroneously categorizes legitimate applicants as high-risk, or fraudulent applications as correct. The fallout could be significant, including a loss of trust, regulatory penalties, and financial instability.

Defending AI systems against data poisoning attacks requires a tailored approach that encompasses meticulous data curation, model robustness, and continuous monitoring.

- **Data Validation and Cleaning:** At the inception of AI model development, thorough data validation and cleaning are paramount. Implementing rigorous quality control measures, outlier detection, and anomaly identification helps identify and isolate potentially poisoned data points. Data validation serves as a good defense against data poisoning attacks by meticulously scrutinizing the quality and authenticity of input data before it enters the training pipeline of an

AI system. This is particularly important when the data being used to train your AI system is outside the control of your organization. Risk analysis should be performed on every input data into your training process, with a particular focus on data you do not control. Mitigating measures should be identified, and decisions on which risks to accept should be taken in the whole context of your AI system. Employing a diverse team in the data curation process can bring in varied perspectives and help identify potential biases or vulnerabilities.

- **Feature Engineering:** Feature engineering is the deliberate crafting and selection of relevant input variables or features that feed into an AI model during its training process. In the context of protecting AI systems against data poisoning attacks, feature engineering assumes a critical role. By carefully selecting features that are inherently resistant to subtle variations or manipulations, such as outliers or anomalies introduced by adversaries, feature engineering acts as a preemptive shield. This strategic selection of features ensures that the AI model focuses on patterns that are genuinely informative and robust, reducing the susceptibility to tainted data points that might attempt to distort the learning process.

- **Regular Model Retraining:** Frequent model retraining with updated and verified data minimizes the impact of potential poisoning attacks. A dynamic learning process allows the model to adapt to evolving attack techniques. By periodically refreshing the model with updated and verified data, organizations create a feedback loop that mitigates the impact of potential poisoning attempts. As attackers evolve their techniques, regular retraining ensures that the

AI system remains attuned to the latest data patterns while discarding any misleading or compromised information. This approach helps the model recalibrate itself, reducing the influence of manipulated data points that adversaries might introduce over time.

- **Data Diversity and Augmentation:** Data augmentation involves artificially expanding the diversity and size of a training dataset by applying controlled transformations to the existing data. A diverse training dataset reduces the effectiveness of data poisoning. By introducing variations such as rotations, translations, or noise to the training data, organizations create a more robust learning environment. This, in turn, enhances the model's ability to generalize and identify patterns amidst potential adversarial manipulations. In the context of data poisoning attacks, data augmentation acts as a countermeasure by minimizing the impact of injected malicious data. As the AI model has learned to accommodate a wider spectrum of inputs through augmentation, the perturbations introduced by attackers become less effective, safeguarding the integrity of the model's training process.

- **Outlier Detection:** Through advanced algorithms and statistical analysis, outlier detection helps segregate tainted data, preventing it from unduly influencing the model's learning process. By actively filtering out anomalies and outliers that could potentially originate from data poisoning attempts, outlier detection ensures that the AI model's training remains centered around genuine and representative data, securing it against deceptive inputs and preserving its accuracy and reliability.

The responsibility falls upon innovative leaders, developers, and cybersecurity experts to craft AI systems that can decipher between authentic and malicious data. By strengthening the AI development lifecycle with data quality checks, robust model architectures, and ongoing vigilance, you can address the risk of data poisoning and embrace the transformative potential of AI while minimizing its inherent risks.

Methodology to Securing AI and ML Systems

"Fix the dang software."
– Gary McGraw, pioneer in software security

AI and ML introduces an unprecedented level of complexity, which creates novel security challenges, demanding innovative strategies and robust defense mechanisms to safeguard against potential threats.

How is protecting AI and ML systems different from other systems?

As we appreciate the capabilities of AI and ML, it is crucial to recognize the unique challenges they bring, especially in terms of security and ethical considerations. Protecting AI and ML systems is fundamentally different from safeguarding traditional IT systems. While standard security measures like access control and addressing software bugs are essential, AI and ML add an extra layer of complexity. The key difference lies in the role of data. In AI and ML systems, data does not just inform the system; it shapes and directs it. Malicious actors can exploit this by manipulating the data, leading to altered or harmful outputs. This can happen in various ways, including interacting with an AI-powered system in real time, tricking it into unexpected behaviors, or targeting the training data, skewing the AI's learning process and outcomes.

A great source of information on the ever-evolving ML attacks is the Berryville Institute of Machine Learning, founded by Gary McGraw. They divide ML attacks into manipulation attacks, which compromise integrity, and extraction attacks, which compromise confidentiality, as follows:

- Input manipulation
- Data manipulation
- Model manipulation
- Input extraction
- Data extraction
- Model extraction

While this approach to defending machine learning (ML) systems may seem a bit academic, it allows for a more comprehensive and systematic exploration of potential security threats. By categorizing attacks into manipulation and extraction, it is possible to dive deeper into each category and identify specific vulnerabilities.

For instance, under manipulation attacks, we find input, data, and model manipulation. Input manipulation involves tweaking the inputs to ML systems to yield desired outputs, while data manipulation targets the data used in training the model. Model manipulation, on the other hand, refers to attacks that aim to alter the model's parameters or structure.

Extraction attacks consist of input, data, and model extraction. In input extraction, an attacker tries to infer sensitive information about the inputs based on the system's outputs. Data extraction involves an attempt to recreate the training data, and model extraction seeks to clone the model itself.

By breaking down the complexity of ML system defense into these distinct categories, we can develop targeted strategies to protect against each type of attack, leading to more robust and secure AI and ML systems. The landscape is constantly evolving, and new threats emerge as technology advances. Hence, a proactive and adaptive approach to AI and ML security is crucial to stay ahead of potential threats.

Adversarial Attacks on AI: Fooling the Machine

"You can fool all the people some of the time, and some of the people all the time, but you cannot fool all the people all the time."
– Abraham Lincoln, 16th president of the United States

Adversarial attacks on artificial intelligence (AI) systems have emerged as a sophisticated and dangerous category of cyberattacks. These attacks specifically target AI models, where attackers craft and manipulate the inputs fed into these systems with the intent to deceive. The goal of such manipulations is to induce erroneous behavior or outputs from the AI, effectively turning its strengths into vulnerabilities.

A notable instance of an adversarial attack was demonstrated by researchers at MIT, where slight alterations to a stop sign made it recognizable as a speed limit sign to an AI-driven autonomous vehicle system. Another example is in health care, where small, undetectable changes in medical imagery led an AI diagnostic system to misdiagnose conditions.

Adversarial attacks exploit the inherent weaknesses and blind spots in the algorithms that underpin AI models. Unlike traditional cyber threats that might target software vulnerabilities or system infrastructure, adversarial attacks focus on the AI's decision-making process itself. These attacks are insidious in nature, as they often involve subtle changes to input data that are imperceptible to humans but significant enough to mislead the AI. For example, a slight alteration in pixel's value in an image can cause an AI image recognition system to mislabel it entirely.

One of the biggest challenges in defending against adversarial attacks is the difficulty in predicting an AI model's behavior in response to these manipulations, both before deployment and during operation. AI models, especially those based on complex algorithms like deep learning, can exhibit unpredictable and non-intuitive behavior in the face of manipulated inputs. This unpredictability is compounded by the fact that AI models often operate as "black boxes," with inner workings that are not fully transparent or understandable, even to the developers.

Unfortunately, adversarial attacks are constantly evolving, causing concern and unease. As AI models become more advanced, so do the techniques used to attack them. Attackers are constantly finding new ways to exploit vulnerabilities, making it a relentless game of cat and mouse between attackers and defenders. Protecting AI systems against these threats requires a deep understanding of both the AI models and the potential attack vectors.

Adversarial attacks present a unique and formidable challenge in AI security, requiring a specialized approach to defense, one that is adaptive, comprehensive, and rooted in a deep understanding of AI technologies and their vulnerabilities.

There are several things that your organization can do to protect systems against these attacks.

- **Input pre-processing:** This technique focuses on refining input data before it reaches the AI model. By normalizing, filtering, and sanitizing data, potentially harmful manipulations can be mitigated. However, this method should not be the sole line of defense. It is most effective when used in conjunction with other strategies.

- **Adversarial training:** This involves exposing AI models to deliberately altered adversarial examples during their training phase. Such exposure helps the model distinguish between genuine and manipulated inputs, enhancing its decision-making abilities. It is crucial to identify and address the system's weak points during this process.

- **Ensemble models**: Leveraging the power of multiple AI models can create a more robust system. If one model falls prey to an attack, the collective decision-making of others can counterbalance the impact. However, this approach requires careful management to avoid overly complex systems, which can impede explainability, a topic explored in depth later.

- **Adversarial robustness training:** Much like stress-testing a bridge's structural integrity once built, this strategy involves rigorously testing AI systems post-development with a variety of adversarial examples to pinpoint and rectify vulnerabilities. It is essential to equip both AI developers and testers with specialized knowledge in adversarial attack methods, distinct from traditional software testing expertise.

Each of these strategies plays a crucial role in protecting AI systems against adversarial attacks. Understanding and implementing these defensive tactics becomes vital for maintaining the integrity and reliability of AI-driven solutions.

Biases in AI and ML: Unintentional Lessons and Their Impact

"Artificial intelligence is just a new tool, one that can be used for good and for bad purposes and one that comes with new dangers and downsides as well. We know already that although machine learning has huge potential, data sets with ingrained biases will produce biased results—garbage in, garbage out."
– Sarah Jeong, American journalist

In 2018, Amazon faced a significant issue with its AI recruiting tool. The tool, designed to automate the job application process, was found to be biased against female candidates. This bias led to female candidates being less likely to be hired. As a result of this discovery, Amazon decided to shut down the project. This example highlights the importance of ethical considerations in data collection, storage, and usage, ensuring that data is utilized responsibly and equitably while respecting the rights and well-being of individuals.

The origin of the phrase, "garbage in, garbage out," is not entirely certain. While the phrase originally related to the computing industry, it has entered the general lexicon, where it is also used to describe failures in human decision-making due to faulty, incomplete, or imprecise data.

This phrase, though old, highlights a crucial element of AI and ML, which is the dependency on data quality. The data that trains AI models significantly shapes their performance and outcomes. However, this data often contains inherent biases, which can unintentionally be transferred into AI systems. These biases might then lead to outcomes that reinforce existing societal inequalities.

Data biases refer to the presence of skewed, unfair, or unrepresentative information within training datasets used to develop AI models. These biases can emerge from various sources, including historical prejudices, cultural stereotypes, or flawed data collection processes. When these biases find their way into AI algorithms, they can perpetuate discriminatory or skewed decision-making, amplifying social disparities and unintentionally endorsing prejudiced behaviors.

Facial recognition systems have shown biases against certain racial groups. For example, some software has been known to misidentify people of specific races, leading to false arrests and unwarranted surveillance. Such outcomes are not due to the AI systems themselves being biased, but rather a reflection of the biases present in the training data.

The repercussions of biased AI systems can be profound. These biases can lead to tangible financial and reputational risks for businesses, as biased algorithms could result in discriminatory products or services, legal liabilities, and damaged brand reputation.

Consider the real-world example of an AI-powered lending platform that unintentionally favored affluent applicants over marginalized ones due to biased training data. This not only led to unjust lending decisions but also attracted negative media coverage, regulatory scrutiny, and financial losses. Ultimately, your organization might fail to do business with a section of the public who might otherwise be good business—losing out on revenue, failing to serve clients effectively, and struggling to gain market share—all because of an underlying bias deeply embedded in your system. This bias is elusive, making it challenging to identify and address.

Beyond technical solutions, the role of interdisciplinary teams in AI development is crucial in combating biases. Involving professionals like ethicists, sociologists, and domain experts in the AI development process ensures a more holistic approach to identifying and addressing biases. These experts can provide valuable insights into the ethical, social, and cultural dimensions of AI, helping to create systems that are technically sound and socially responsible. Diverse perspectives can uncover subtle biases that might be overlooked by a purely technical team, leading to more equitable and ethical AI solutions.

Luckily, there are actions you can take to address this issue! Ensuring AI systems are protected against data biases requires a comprehensive approach that encompasses data collection, preprocessing, algorithm design, and ongoing monitoring. Here are some key strategies to mitigate biases.

Diverse and Representative Data

The foundation of unbiased AI is diverse and representative data. The quality of an AI system's predictions hinges upon the inclusivity of its training data. By incorporating a wide spectrum of demographic, cultural, and socio-economic perspectives, developers can mitigate the risk of unintentional biases permeating their models. Diverse data ensures that the AI system is exposed to a comprehensive range of scenarios, reducing the likelihood of it favoring one group over another. An important exercise to do is to identify which biases your training data might have.

Data Preprocessing

Careful preprocessing of training data can help reduce biases. Techniques like data augmentation, anonymization, and removing irrelevant features can minimize biases in the input data and make it clearer where your biases might be.

Data augmentation involves artificially increasing the variety and amount of data in the training set. It is achieved by making controlled modifications to existing data to generate new, diverse examples. For instance, in image recognition tasks, augmentation might include flipping, rotating, or altering the colors of images. This helps the model learn from a broader range of inputs, improving its ability to generalize and reducing overfitting to specific traits in the training data.

Anonymization refers to the process of removing or altering personally identifiable information from a dataset. The goal is to protect individual privacy while maintaining the usefulness of the data. Techniques include masking, pseudonymization (replacing private identifiers with fake identifiers or pseudonyms), and data aggregation (combining data in a way that individual data points cannot be distinguished). Anonymization is crucial in datasets that contain sensitive information, ensuring that the data can be used for training without compromising individual privacy or confidentiality. When implemented incorrectly, anonymization has the potential to modify the behavior of your model. Therefore, it is crucial to execute this process with utmost care and precision.

Algorithmic Fairness

AI developers should incorporate fairness metrics during algorithm design to identify and rectify biases. Techniques like re-sampling, re-weighting, and adversarial training can be used to mitigate biases in the model's predictions.

Re-sampling involves modifying the training dataset to balance representation across different groups. For instance, if a dataset has an underrepresentation of a certain demographic, re-sampling can be used to increase the prevalence of data from that group. This can be achieved either by oversampling underrepresented groups or under sampling overrepresented ones, thus creating a more balanced dataset that helps reduce bias.

Re-weighting adjusts the importance (or weight) given to different samples in the training dataset. If certain groups are underrepresented, their data points can be assigned greater weight, ensuring the model pays more attention to these during training. This technique helps in training the model on a more equitable basis, mitigating biases that may arise from unbalanced datasets.

Adversarial training is where the model is exposed to adversarial examples, or data points specifically designed to challenge and "trick" the model. This method can be used to identify and correct biases by including adversarial examples that represent minority groups or other underrepresented categories. The model then learns to make decisions that are more generalizable and less biased towards the majority group represented in the training data.

By implementing these techniques, AI developers contribute to building technology that aligns with ethical standards and respects the rights and dignity of every individual, fostering a world where AI operates as a force for good without amplifying societal biases.

Regular Auditing, Monitoring, and Adaptation

Regularly audit AI systems for bias and fairness post-deployment. This involves analyzing system outputs across different demographic groups and identifying potential discrepancies. Regular auditing not only reinforces the system's fairness but also fosters accountability and transparency, as organizations demonstrate a commitment to upholding ethical standards and rectifying any inadvertent biases that may arise in AI deployments.

Biases are constantly evolving, shaping our perceptions and judgments. Continuous monitoring and adaptation of AI systems will be necessary to ensure they remain as unbiased as possible as new data emerges.

As AI and ML continue to shape our world, understanding and addressing biases in these technologies is important. Data biases pose a substantial threat, capable of perpetuating social injustices, damaging reputations, and eroding trust. By diligently implementing strategies that emphasize diverse data collection, preprocessing, algorithmic fairness, and ongoing monitoring, innovative leaders can minimize AI system biases, fostering a future where technology plays a role in promoting equality rather than reinforcing discrimination.

The Importance of Explainability in AI and ML

"An explanation not only solves the puzzle but also illuminates the path of learning."
— Carl Sagan, astronomer

The Correctional Offender Management Profiling for Alternative Sanctions (COMPAS) algorithm is a controversial tool that is used by courts to make bail decisions in the United States. The algorithm is designed to assess the risk of reoffending by criminal defendants.

A 2016 study by ProPublica found that the COMPAS algorithm was biased against black defendants. The study found that black defendants were more likely to be classified as high-risk and to be denied bail, even though they were no more likely to reoffend than white defendants.

A general critique of the use of proprietary software such as COMPAS is that since the algorithms it uses are trade secrets, they cannot be examined by the public and affected parties, which may be a violation of due process. The ProPublica study highlighted the dangers of using AI systems that are not explainable.

As organizations integrate AI and ML technologies into various aspects of their operations, a new set of challenges and concerns has emerged. One of the most crucial among these is the concept of explainability, a fundamental element in ensuring the trustworthiness and reliability of AI and ML systems.

Explainability is the ability of an AI or ML model to provide clear and understandable insights into its decision-making processes. It involves unraveling the complex web of computations, data inputs, and algorithms that contribute to the outcomes generated by these systems.

In traditional software applications, understanding the logic behind the code is relatively straightforward. However, AI and ML models often operate in a "black box" manner, where the internal workings are opaque and convoluted, even to the developers who created them. This lack of transparency has raised significant concerns, especially in high-stakes applications such as autonomous vehicles, medical diagnosis, financial decision-making, and criminal justice systems.

When the rationale behind an AI-driven decision cannot be ascertained, it becomes challenging to trust or even validate its outcomes. Explainability is not just an academic concern. It has far-reaching implications for businesses, individuals, and society as a whole. Here are some of the key reasons why explainability holds immense value in AI and ML systems.

- **Trust and Accountability:** Trust is the cornerstone of any technology adoption. When AI systems make decisions that impact human lives, jobs, and well-being, it is imperative to understand the reasoning behind those decisions. Explainable AI provides the necessary insight for individuals to trust that the system is operating fairly and ethically. In cases of erroneous or biased outcomes, accountability can be established by analyzing the decision-making process.

- **Regulatory Compliance:** In recent years, regulatory bodies have started to mandate the use of explainable AI in certain sectors. Non-compliance can lead to hefty fines and reputational damage. Regulations will be covered in more detail later in this chapter.

- **Bias Mitigation:** AI and ML systems are susceptible to inheriting biases present in their training data. These biases can perpetuate discrimination and inequality when making decisions. Explainability allows data scientists and researchers to identify and rectify biases by revealing which features or data points are driving certain outcomes, enabling a more inclusive and equitable technology landscape.

- **Continuous Improvement:** Explainability provides developers with insights into model behavior and performance. This knowledge is invaluable for refining and optimizing the system over time. Whether it is improving accuracy, reducing false positives, or enhancing user experience, explainability facilitates a feedback loop that drives ongoing enhancement.

- **User Adoption:** When end-users, whether employees or customers, understand why an AI system suggests a particular action or decision, they are more likely to embrace it. User adoption is crucial for the success of any AI implementation, and explainability plays a pivotal role in achieving this.

While the benefits of explainability are clear, achieving it is no simple feat. The very nature of AI and ML models, characterized by their complexity and non-linearity, presents challenges in providing simple, human-understandable explanations. Striking a balance between transparency and the inherent complexity of these systems is an ongoing challenge.

Global Regulations

Globally, there is an increasing emphasis on AI explainability in regulations. The EU's GDPR has provisions for the "right to explanation" for AI decisions. In the USA, initiatives like the Algorithmic Accountability Act propose transparency in AI decision-making. Industries like health care and finance are seeing stricter compliance requirements for explainable AI, ensuring fairness and accountability in automated decisions.

The importance of AI explainability is evident in several regulations and guidelines, including:

- **The European Union's Artificial Intelligence Act (AIA):** The AIA regulation sets out a comprehensive framework for the development and use of AI in the European Union. The AIA requires developers of certain high-risk AI systems to provide explanations of their systems' decision-making processes.

- **The United States' National Institute of Standards and Technology's (NIST) Explainable AI (XAI) Guidelines:** The NIST XAI Guidelines are a set of guidelines that provide a framework for developing and evaluating XAI techniques. The guidelines recommend that XAI techniques should be transparent, interpretable, and accountable.

- **The Organization for Economic Co-operation and Development's (OECD) Recommendation on Artificial Intelligence:** The OECD Recommendation on AI is a non-binding recommendation that sets out principles for the development and use of AI. The OECD recommends that AI systems should be explainable to build trust and transparency.

In addition to these regulations and guidelines, there are several industry standards and best practices for AI explainability. These include:

- The Society of Automotive Engineers (SAE) International's J3016 Standard is a standard for explainability of autonomous vehicles. The standard defines a set of requirements for explaining the decision-making processes of autonomous vehicles.

- The Financial Conduct Authority's (FCA) Principles for Machine Learning are a set of principles that apply to the use of machine learning in financial services. The principles recommend that firms should be able to explain how their machine learning systems make decisions.

- The AI for Social Good Alliance's Fair, Transparent, and Accountable (FTA) Principles are a set of principles for the development and use of AI for social good. The principles recommend that AI systems should be explainable and accountable to ensure that they are fair, transparent, and responsible.

Model Cards

In response to the challenges of AI transparency and explainability, model cards have been proposed. Model cards are short documents that accompany trained machine learning models, designed to provide key information about the model.

The purpose of a model card is to increase transparency by communicating information about trained models to a broad audience. They help in promoting explainability and achieving transparency in the use of AI.

A model card typically contains the following information:

- **Context of Use:** Details about the scenarios in which the model is intended to be used.

- **Performance Evaluation:** Information about the model's performance, including metrics and evaluation procedures.

- **Training Data:** Details about the data used to train the model.

- **Model Architecture:** Information about the construction of the machine learning model.

Model cards can be beneficial to various stakeholders. For instance, AI practitioners can learn how a model would work for its intended use cases, developers can compare a model's results to other models created for the same or a similar purpose, and policymakers can understand how a model will impact individuals affected by their policies.

In essence, model cards serve as a form of "nutrition label" for AI models, providing essential facts and promoting responsible use. They are a step towards responsible AI governance, balancing innovation with transparency.

As AI technology continues to develop, it is likely that there will be more regulations and guidelines on AI explainability. This is because explainability is increasingly important for building trust and transparency in AI systems.

Methodology for Achieving Explainability

Different AI techniques might require different approaches to achieve explainability. For instance, traditional rule-based systems might be easier to explain compared to neural networks, which operate as interconnected layers of nodes. Researchers and practitioners are continually exploring techniques like Local Interpretable Model-Agnostic Explanations (LIME) and SHapley Additive exPlanations (SHAP) to generate post hoc explanations for complex models.

LIME is a model-agnostic technique that provides local, interpretable explanations for complex models. It works by approximating the behavior of a complex model in a local region around a specific data point. LIME then fits a simpler model to the local region and uses this model to explain the behavior of the complex model.

SHAP, on the other hand, is a model-specific technique that provides global explanations for complex models. It works by assigning a value to each feature in a model based on its contribution to the model's output. SHAP then uses these feature values to explain the behavior of the model.

Explainability of AI and ML systems is a vital component for fostering trust, accountability, compliance, and overall progress. As organizations embrace these transformative technologies, they must also shoulder the responsibility of ensuring that their AI systems can be understood by both technical experts and non-experts alike. Just as a well-written codebase is essential for traditional software, a transparent and explainable decision-making process is indispensable for AI systems. By championing explainability, businesses and leaders can steer the course of AI and ML innovation while safeguarding against potential pitfalls and building a safer, more equitable technological future.

Artificial General Intelligence: Navigating the Future of Intelligent Systems

"We have no more reason to think that a sufficiently advanced machine intelligence would share our ultimate values than we have to think that it would care about our welfare or any other aspect of our existence."
– Nick Bostrom, author of *Superintelligence: Paths, Dangers, Strategies*

Artificial general intelligence (AGI) represents a paradigm shift from today's AI, which excels in narrow, specific tasks. AGI is envisioned as possessing the ability to understand, learn, and apply intelligence across a wide range of cognitive tasks at or above human level. It is a theoretical form of AI that can adaptively reason and solve problems in various domains, demonstrating creativity, social intelligence, and general wisdom.

Futurist Ray Kurzweil forecasted that the 2040s might witness the emergence of AGI, with machines exhibiting intelligence indistinguishable from humans. This projection is rooted in the Law of Accelerating Returns, which assumes exponential growth in technologies like computing and AI. Bostrom, however, offers a more conservative view, noting that predicting the arrival of AGI is fraught with uncertainty. Essential technological milestones on the path to AGI include:

- **Advanced Neural Networks:** The evolution of neural networks to mimic the complexity and efficiency of the human brain is a crucial aspect of AGI development. However, some argue that deep neural networks alone may not be sufficient to achieve AGI.

- **Quantum Computing:** Quantum computing, with its ability to process vast amounts of data and solve complex problems rapidly, could significantly accelerate the development of AGI.

- **Sophisticated natural language processing (NLP):** The creation of NLP systems that can truly comprehend and interpret human language with all its subtleties is a significant step towards AGI.

- **Human-AI Collaboration:** The development of systems where AI and humans can learn from and enhance each other is seen as a foundational step for more advanced AI capabilities.

AGI poses profound ethical and existential risks. The "alignment problem" is central, involving aligning AGI's goals and decisions with human ethics and values. Unaligned AGI could pursue objectives harmful to humanity, intentionally or inadvertently. Bostrom warns of the "control problem," which is how to control superintelligent systems once they surpass human intelligence. The ethical implications of AGI are complex, ranging from concerns about autonomous decision-making in warfare to societal impacts like job displacement and privacy. It is crucial to establish ethical frameworks and guidelines that govern the development and deployment of AGI, ensuring that these systems are aligned with human values and societal norms. Collaborative efforts between technologists, ethicists, policymakers, and the public are essential to addressing ethical challenges of AGI.

The introduction of AGI will transform the cybersecurity landscape. AGI systems could be exploited to launch sophisticated cyberattacks, potentially leading to unprecedented scales of disruption. The security of AGI systems themselves is another concern, as their complex decision-making processes might be opaque, making it difficult to predict and defend against vulnerabilities.

Mitigating AGI risks requires a holistic approach:

- **Robust and Safe AI Design:** Developing AGI systems with fail-safe mechanisms and ethical decision-making processes.

- **Interdisciplinary Research:** Collaboration between AI researchers, ethicists, sociologists, and policymakers to understand and address the multifaceted implications of AGI.

- **Global AI Ethics and Policies:** Establishing universally accepted ethical guidelines and policies for AGI development and application.

- **Continuous Oversight and Evaluation:** Implementing systems for continuous monitoring and evaluation of AGI impacts, with the flexibility to adapt policies and strategies as AGI evolves.

Regulatory frameworks for AGI are in their infancy. The European Union's approach to AI regulation, focusing on high-risk applications, could be a model for future AGI governance. Countries like the USA, China, and members of the OECD are also starting to consider the implications of advanced AI systems. A global dialogue and consensus are essential, given AGI's potential global impact.

AGI offers immense potential benefits, from revolutionizing health care and environmental management, to transforming education and the economy. However, it also poses risks like exacerbating social inequalities, displacing jobs, and creating new forms of digital divide. A thoughtful, inclusive approach to AGI development is crucial to harness its benefits while mitigating its risks.

Chapter 4

Robots Among Us:
Safeguarding the Age of Robotics

"We humans have a love-hate relationship with our technology.
We love each new advance, and we hate how fast our world is changing...
The robots really embody that love-hate relationship we have with technology."
– Daniel H. Wilson, author of *Robopocalypse*

A Robot's World: The Dawn of Robotics

*"A.I. will make it possible for the internet to directly engage people
in the real world, through robotics and drones and little machines
that will do smart things by themselves."*
– Jensen Huang, co-founder, president, and CEO of NVIDEA

In October 2023, Amazon was reported to be rolling out expanded robotics operations at fulfillment centers built on updated sorting machines, robotic arms, and its Roomba-like mover bots. The company's Sparrow robot arm can identify products inside totes and pull them out, while the autonomous Proteus and Hercules robots that roll around like those home robot vacuums, can lift and move shelves, distribute containers, and deliver products in the building so humans do not have to. Such advancements are optimizing Amazon's operations and setting a precedent for the future of automation in supply chain logistics.

This is just one of many organizations developing and deploying robotics in their operations. This trend is expected to continue. The International Federation of Robotics cites, in the World Robotics 2023 report, that there were approximately 553k industrial robot installations in factories around the world, a growth rate of 5% in 2022, year on year. By region, 73% of all newly deployed robots were installed in Asia, 15% in Europe, and 10% in the Americas.

Beyond Amazon's robotics operations, the field of robotics has made significant strides in diverse sectors. In health care, robots assist in surgeries with precision beyond human capabilities, while in agriculture, they revolutionize farming practices with automated harvesting and monitoring systems. These examples illustrate the versatile and transformative nature of robotics across various industries.

But before you get excited, let's step back and look at a few definitions and a brief history of robotics.

A Brief Definition of Robotics

Imagine you have a series of tasks that are repetitive, monotonous, dangerous, or require high precision. Think about assembling car parts in a factory, defusing a bomb, performing a complex surgical procedure, or even vacuuming your home. These are all tasks that robots can easily perform.

At its core, a robot is a machine that is designed to do things that would otherwise be done by humans. But what sets a robot apart from other machines is its ability to interact with the world in an intelligent and autonomous way. This means that a robot can sense its environment, process information, make decisions, and act accordingly, without human intervention.

There are three major elements to robotics, which scientists and engineers work on:

- **Perception:** Robots are equipped with sensors to understand their surroundings. This can be anything from cameras that help a robot see, to infrared sensors that let a robot detect heat, or even ultrasonic sensors that allow a robot to measure distance using sound waves.

- **Processing:** Once a robot has sensed its environment, it needs to understand what it is perceiving. This is where computer programming and artificial intelligence become relevant. These technologies allow a robot to turn raw sensor data into meaningful information, and to make decisions based on that information.

- **Action:** After a robot has perceived its environment and decided, it needs to act. Robots interact with the world through devices called actuators. Depending on the robot, these could be motors that turn wheels, robotic arms that pick objects up, or speakers that allow a robot to communicate verbally.

Robotics is about creating machines that can function intelligently and independently in a variety of environments, thereby augmenting human capabilities, improving efficiency, and ensuring safety. It is a fascinating field that is constantly evolving and becoming more integral to our lives.

A Brief History of Robotics

The journey of robotics is a fascinating one, which began as far back as 1495 with Leonardo da Vinci's humanoid robot sketch. The term "robot" itself was introduced by Karel Čapek in his play R.U.R. in 1920, and Isaac Asimov outlined the well-known "Three Laws of Robotics" in 1942.

The first programmable robot, Unimate, was patented by George Devol in 1954, and installed on a General Motors assembly line in 1961. In 1965, Robert Lee introduced homogeneous transformation, a mathematical concept used in robotics, particularly in the fields of robot motion planning and control.

The Stanford Arm, an electrically powered, programmable robotic arm with six degrees of freedom, was designed by Professor Victor Scheinman in the 1970s. In 1982, GM and FANUC formed GM Fanuc Robotics Corporation, one of the world's largest industrial robot manufacturers.

Throughout the late 20th century, academic and corporate investment in robotics surged, leading to remarkable breakthroughs.

The Carnegie Mellon University Robotics Institute was established in 1994, bolstering academic research in robotics. NASA's Mars Pathfinder mission, which included the Sojourner rover, marked a monumental moment in space robotics in 1997.

In the 21st century, robotics has become far more complex and more interesting. Honda revealed ASIMO, an advanced humanoid robot, in 2000, and iRobot released the Roomba vacuum cleaner in 2002. Boston

Dynamics made headlines with its dynamically balanced, walking robots in 2005.

Rethink Robotics introduced Baxter, a milestone in collaborative robotics, in 2012. Hanson Robotics unveiled Sophia, a humanoid robot capable of natural language conversations, in 2016, and Boston Dynamics released the SpotMini robot in 2017.

Neura Robotics is a German startup that since 2019 has been building cognitive robots, machines that possess memory and the ability to operate across a complex and changing mix of variables and can collaborate with people ("cobots" as Neura calls them). Cobots have additional features, allowing them to safely work with and alongside humans.

Optimus, also known as the Tesla Bot, was announced at Tesla's Artificial Intelligence (AI) Day on 19 August 2021. Tesla CEO Elon Musk presented the latest prototype of Optimus at a Silicon Valley event in October 2022. A video of Optimus was shown performing simple tasks, such as watering plants, carrying boxes, and lifting metal bars.

Optimus is designed to address labor shortages and enhance workplace safety. It is designed to perform unsafe, repetitive, or boring tasks. The aim is to create a general-purpose, bi-pedal, autonomous humanoid robot. Musk stated that the robots could be produced en masse, at a cost lower than $20,000.

The field of robotics has evolved in tandem with societal needs and technological breakthroughs. From the mechanical automatons of ancient civilizations to the advanced AI-driven robots of today, the journey of robotics mirrors humanity's quest for innovation and efficiency. This historical perspective enriches our understanding of robotics and highlights its transformative role in shaping our future.

Exploring the Contradictions and Paradoxes in Robotics

Have you ever come across one of those cleaning robots and found yourself unable to resist pausing and gazing in wonder. What will it do next? Will it function flawlessly? Or will it encounter a mishap? Robots have the power to captivate our imagination and ignite our curiosity. Yet, alongside these marvels, arise numerous paradoxes that challenge conventional assumptions.

- **The Autonomy Paradox:** As we push for robots to be more autonomous, a curious phenomenon emerges. The more independent a robot becomes, the greater our need to supervise, manage, and decipher its actions. This paradox springs from a critical need to ensure that robots align with our ethical, safety, and operational norms. So, oddly enough, the journey towards robotic independence amplifies humanity's role in overseeing and maintaining these machines.

  The autonomy paradox is aptly highlighted in drone surveillance, where increased robotic autonomy in monitoring tasks requires sophisticated oversight mechanisms to ensure ethical and legal compliance.

- **Moravec's Paradox:** This paradox turns our intuitive understanding of complexity on its head. Coined by pioneers like Hans Moravec,

Rodney Brooks, and Marvin Minsky, this observation highlights that tasks we deem intellectually challenging, such as high-level mathematics, are quite simple for robots or machines. On the flip side, what we consider instinctive, like recognizing objects or a simple walk in the park, can stump the most advanced robots.

Why this discrepancy? Moravec posits that our intellectual abilities have evolved recently and are more "conscious," making them easier to program. However, instinctual abilities, perfected over millennia, operate subconsciously, making them computationally heavy to reproduce. This paradox underscores why a robot can defeat us in a game of Go, yet struggle with tasks a toddler accomplishes with ease.

Moravec's Paradox is especially evident in autonomous vehicles, as these vehicles struggle to navigate complex environments that humans find instinctual.

- **The Uncanny Valley:** In our quest to humanize robots, we have stumbled upon an eerie territory. The closer robots resemble us, with slight imperfections, the more they unsettle us. This phenomenon, termed the "uncanny valley," asserts that almost-perfect humanoid robots can elicit feelings of discomfort or even revulsion in humans. In trying to mirror humanity, we inadvertently amplify the artificial aspects, making the machines appear eerier. The very pursuit of anthropomorphic perfection in robotics might, paradoxically, be what repels us from them.

These paradoxes are not mere quirks; they shape our understanding, development, and interaction with robots. As the robotics industry

www.BookOnCybersecurity.com

develops further, these insights serve as a reminder that mastering robotics is as much about understanding ourselves as it is about the machines.

The robotics industry continues to intersect with fields such as artificial intelligence, materials science, nanotechnology, and biotechnology, pushing the boundaries of what is possible. Robots are becoming an integral part of our lives, enhancing our capabilities, improving our efficiency, and offering exciting possibilities for the future.

Hijacking the Helpers:
The Threat of Robot Malware

"If a robot can be manipulated into doing harm to a man,
one might say we ought to make the human better. That is impossible,
so we will make the robot more foolproof."
– Isaac Asimov, author

As robots have become more prevalent, a new cybersecurity threat has surfaced, namely robot malware. Robots have moved from being mere tools to potential cybersecurity targets. Hospitals, manufacturing lines, delivery services, and our homes have all seen the integration of robotic assistance. As with all technologies, where there is connectivity, there is vulnerability.

In 2017, researchers at the security firm Trend Micro and Italy's Politecnico Milano demonstrated how hackers could sabotage an industrial robotic arm. They developed attack techniques that could subtly sabotage and even fully hijack a 220-pound industrial robotic arm capable of wielding gripping claws, welding tools, or lasers, causing it to damage the products it manufactures or potentially harm human operators. While this was a controlled experiment conducted by security researchers, it illustrates the potential of a cyberattack. Frighteningly, the compromised robot has broad usage, from automotive manufacturing to food processing, packaging, and pharmaceuticals, amongst others. The researchers commented that if they were able to find so many basic security flaws in this specific robot, then other industrial robots will be vulnerable to similar attacks.

This example underscores the urgency of safeguarding robots. Cybersecurity for robots is indeed an important issue that needs ongoing attention as these technologies continue to evolve and become more integrated into our daily lives.

Considering the impact of robot malware in a health care environment, especially when robots have vital responsibilities in patient care, highlights the seriousness of this threat. A breach in this context could lead to medical errors or violations of patient privacy, making the development of robust cybersecurity measures in robotics a technical necessity and moral imperative.

Understanding robot malware requires a look into its mechanisms. Robots, like computers, operate based on software. When this software is tampered with, the robot's actions can deviate from its intended function. Hackers may interfere with inputs by feeding misleading data to a robot's sensors, inducing faulty actions; corrupt decision-making algorithms to alter the logic by which a robot operates, resulting in drastic consequences; and manipulate actuators, by controlling a robot's physical movements, harming or disrupting operators.

The complexity arises from the intertwined nature of modern robotics. Robots mostly do not work in isolation but are part of a connected ecosystem. This interconnectivity, while enabling efficient operations, also provides multiple entry points for malicious actors.

To address the threat, robot developers and manufacturers should continue to commit resources into securing robot defenses. Efforts should include:

- **Embedded Security by Design:** By building security into the architecture and design of robots, manufacturers can develop a foundational layer of protection.

- **Real-time Monitoring:** Detecting anomalies in robot behavior allows for swift intervention before any significant harm can ensue.

- **Secure Communication Channels:** Encrypting communication between robots and control centers cuts off a prime vulnerability point.

The field of robotics, while promising in its applications and innovations, cannot afford to neglect the cybersecurity challenges. But challenges breed solutions. While not specifically relating to cybersecurity of robots, the International Standards Organization (ISO) has defined several standards for robotics:

ISO 10218-1:2011: This standard specifies requirements and guidelines for the inherent safe design, protective measures, and information for use of industrial robots.

- **ISO/TS 15066:2016:** This technical specification specifies safety requirements for collaborative industrial robot systems and the work environment. It supplements the requirements and guidance on collaborative industrial robot operation given in ISO 10218-1 and ISO 10218-2.

- **ISO 22166-1:2021:** This is an International Standard on robot modularity and robot module interoperability focusing on main issues of safety, security, connectivity (from both hardware and software perspectives), and functionality.

- **ISO/TC 299:** The International Organization for Standardization (ISO) Technical Committee 299 develops high-quality standards for the safety of industrial robots and service robots.

In popular culture, the idea of rogue robots is an old trope. Sci-fi classics have long explored this theme, urging humanity to tread with caution. However, the true battle is not against robots but those who seek to misuse them. As robots become increasingly sophisticated, ensuring that they are secured is paramount to ensuring that robots remain our allies and do not turn into adversaries.

Robot malware presents a multifaceted challenge, intertwining technology, ethics, and societal implications. As we integrate robots further into our lives, the onus falls upon developers, regulators, and users alike to ensure their safe and reliable operation.

Securing the Robotics Supply Chain: From Production to Operation

"If you think of standardization as the best that you know today, but which is to be improved tomorrow, you get somewhere."
— Henry Ford, founder of Ford Motor company and developer of the assembly line technique of mass production

Robots are complex, sophisticated marvels of modern engineering. The mass production of robots, which involves numerous components, relies on a sophisticated supply chain that includes everything from sourcing raw materials, manufacturing parts, assembly, and software development, to delivering the final product to consumers. The complexity and interconnectedness of the supply chain poses significant risks. Any interference with an element of the supply chain can result in significant and wide-ranging repercussions.

The robotics supply chain can be divided into three main stages: production, transportation, and operation. Each of these stages presents unique challenges and opportunities for potential vulnerabilities to be exploited. To secure the entire supply chain, it is necessary to address each stage individually.

Production

The production stage involves the design, manufacturing, and assembly of various components to create a functioning robot. Some of the elements of the supply chain during production include:

- **Material Sourcing:** Raw materials, like metals, plastics, or electronic components, are sourced globally. Their quality and integrity are paramount for the robot's durability and performance.

- **Component Manufacturing:** Various components, like sensors, actuators, and processors, are often manufactured in specialized facilities scattered around the world.

- **Assembly:** The amalgamation of components into a functioning robot requires precision, often involving both human expertise and automation.

- **Software Integration:** A robot's "brain," its software, involves multiple software providers and continuous updates.

- **Testing and Quality Assurance:** Before deployment, robots undergo rigorous testing to ensure they operate safely and efficiently.

To give you a sense of how troubling and complex this can be, consider microchips, which are critical to the operation of all computers and robots. Microchips are essential to virtually every digital product and service powering your modern life. These essential components can and do have vulnerabilities, as illustrated in the following cases.

In recent years, a vulnerability known as the branch history injection (BHI) was discovered in both Intel and ARM chips. This vulnerability bypassed certain mitigations, enabling exploits that could leak sensitive data, such as passwords. The affected chips included all of Intel's processors using the Haswell architecture from 2013 onwards, as well as various ARM chips.

Another vulnerability, dubbed "Downfall," was found in Intel chips. This flaw could allow attackers to steal sensitive details like private messages, passwords, and encryption keys. The vulnerability affected several Intel chip families produced between 2015 and 2021.

While software vulnerabilities in microchips, as previously discussed, are troubling, the hardware side of things is not exempt from risks. The vulnerabilities intrinsic to the design of the hardware can sometimes pose even more significant threats, especially since they can be harder to patch without physical replacements or significant updates.

Take, for instance, the Meltdown and Spectre vulnerabilities. Discovered in 2018, these vulnerabilities are present in most microprocessors manufactured by various companies. They exploit critical vulnerabilities in modern processors, allowing unauthorized users to read sensitive data in the system's memory, which might include passwords, encryption keys, or sensitive information in open applications.

Meltdown primarily affects Intel processors and works by breaking the mechanism that keeps applications from accessing arbitrary system memory. This could potentially allow an attacker to access data from other programs and the operating system.

Spectre, on the other hand, is more insidious. It affects Intel, AMD, and ARM processors and can trick vulnerable applications into leaking secrets. Instead of directly attacking memory, Spectre exploits the process of speculative execution, a technique used by modern processors to optimize performance.

Both vulnerabilities underscore the challenges in securing the robotics supply chain. While software issues can often be patched with updates, hardware vulnerabilities like Meltdown and Spectre require more involved solutions, sometimes even needing hardware replacements. As robots increasingly become integral to industries and personal spaces, understanding, and addressing both hardware and software vulnerabilities is paramount.

Given the production supply chain risks, it is essential to ensure secure and reliable sourcing of materials and components. Quality control measures must be in place at every stage of production, with adherence to strict standards for safety, performance, and security.

Transportation

Once robots are produced, they need to be transported from the manufacturing facility to their intended destination. During this stage, physical security measures are essential. Some steps that can be taken include:

- **Tamper-proof Packaging:** Using packaging materials that cannot be easily opened or tampered with during transportation can help prevent unauthorized access.

- **GPS Tracking:** Installing GPS tracking devices on containers can provide real-time location updates and alerts if there are any deviations from the planned route.

- **Limited Access:** Restricting access to transportation vehicles and containers can minimize the risk of theft or sabotage.

Operation

The final stage in the supply chain is the operation of robots. This is when they are used, either in industrial settings or as personal service robots. With their increased connectivity, it is crucial to implement robust cybersecurity measures at this stage, such as:

- **Network Segmentation:** Separating the network used for robot operations from other networks can limit the spread of malware and isolate potential threats.

- **Regular Updates:** Keeping software and firmware updated will patch any discovered vulnerabilities that may be exploited by attackers.

- **Secure Communication Protocols:** Encrypting communication channels between robots and control centers can prevent unauthorized access to sensitive data.

Considering the numerous challenges faced by the robotics supply chain, what steps can be taken to address them effectively?

To ensure the security and efficacy of the robotic supply chain, several measures are recommended:

- **Transparency and Traceability:** Modern technologies like blockchain can track every element of a robot's journey, from inception to delivery, guaranteeing accountability at each stage. Blockchain's decentralized nature ensures data integrity, making it an ideal solution for enhancing transparency in the supply chain.

- **Vendor Verification:** Regularly vetting and monitoring suppliers ensures the quality and authenticity of components. This process can be automated using AI-based systems that can analyze supplier performance data in real time.

- **End-to-End Encryption:** Protecting communication within the supply chain, especially concerning software, prevents unauthorized access and tampering. Advanced encryption algorithms and secure communication protocols can be employed to safeguard data transmission.

- **Regular Audits:** Periodic checks and evaluations of the entire supply chain can identify and rectify weak points. These audits can be facilitated by predictive analytics tools that can detect anomalies and potential risks.

- **Collaborative Standards:** Industry-wide standards can create a uniformity of security protocols, ensuring all participants uphold certain security measures.

By implementing these measures, the robotics supply chain can be fortified against potential threats, ensuring smooth operation from production to delivery.

Securing the robotics supply chain is a continuous process that requires cooperation and collaboration between all parties involved. As technology evolves, so do the methods used by cyberattackers. It is essential to stay vigilant and continuously improve security measures to keep up with these threats. By implementing secure design practices, robust supply chain management protocols, and strong cybersecurity measures during production, transportation, and operation, you can ensure the safe and reliable use of robots.

Securing Robot Communication: Guarding the Information Exchange

*"The single biggest problem in communication
is the illusion that it has taken place."*
— George Bernard Shaw, playwright

In a bustling hospital in Tokyo, a robot named Hiro swiftly navigates corridors, delivering medicine to patients. Hiro is not just following a predefined path; it is communicating in real time with other robots and the hospital's central system. In today's world, seamless robot communication like Hiro's is a necessity, and the foundation of such communication is security. With robots making critical contributions across diverse sectors, compromised communication might mean a delay in medication or graver scenarios, like a national security threat.

There are a few fundamental things to consider when thinking about communication between robots. At its core, communication involves the exchange of information between two or more entities. In the case of robots, this data can include commands, sensor readings, and even location updates. Fundamentally, robot communication can be categorized in the following ways:

- Robot-to-Robot (R2R) communication is two robots talking to each other, sharing information, and collaborating without humans. It is like two friends passing notes in class, but for robots, the notes are instructions, data, and status updates to get a job done. Picture a factory where robots collaboratively assemble a car. They constantly exchange data, synchronize movements, and adapt strategies.

- Robot-to-Infrastructure (R2I) communication is when robots connect to systems and networks around them, like a computer checking in with the internet. For robots, this means getting instructions, sending updates, or syncing with things like traffic lights or hospital databases to do their tasks better. For example, a drone, after completing its surveillance mission, connects to a cloud system, uploading its findings and downloading software updates.

In practice, secure communication protocols such as message queuing telemetry transport (MQTT) and data distribution service (DDS) are increasingly adopted in robotics for their robustness and reliability. Emerging technologies like blockchain are also being explored for enhancing the security and integrity of robot communications.

Equipped with a basic understanding of how robots communicate, consider the potential cybersecurity challenges that threaten to undermine these sophisticated systems.

- **Interception:** In a world where information is as valuable as currency, the transmission of unencrypted data is a major vulnerability. For example, a robot holding the blueprints to a new, groundbreaking design. If these plans were transmitted without proper encryption, they could be intercepted and fall into the hands of competitors. The consequence would be a significant loss of market advantage and an erosion of the innovation edge that organizations work so tirelessly to maintain.

- **Tampering:** It is not difficult to envision a scenario where a security robot, entrusted with the safety of a facility, is manipulated to overlook a breach. This could be as simple as altering the robot's programming to ignore certain signals, thereby leaving what was once a secure facility open to threats. The implications range from stolen assets to compromised personal safety, all resulting from a single point of failure in the robot's cybersecurity protocols.

- **Data Injection:** This form of cyberattack can have catastrophic effects in sectors such as agriculture. Imagine an agricultural robot that has been fed falsified sensor data, leading it to misidentify thriving crops as invasive weeds. The robot, operating under the guise of efficiency, could inadvertently destroy an entire season's yield, causing economic damage and disrupting the food supply chain.

Some of the specific cybersecurity controls worth considering for robotics communications include:

- **End-to-End Encryption:** Encrypting communication channels between robots prevents eavesdropping.

- **Authentication Protocols:** Ensuring that navigation commands received by robots come from trusted sources is crucial.

- **Adopting Secure Network Protocols:** Implementing robust protocols is vital to safeguard data exchange in robotic networks.

- **Messaging Protocols:** Message queuing telemetry transport (MQTT) and data distribution service (DDS) are secure communication protocols specifically designed for the efficient transmission of data in robotic and IoT environments. These protocols are favored for their ability to handle high volumes of data with minimal latency and for their reliability in maintaining secure connections.

- **Blockchain Technology:** The use of blockchain in robotic communications is an emerging trend. Its decentralized nature can enhance the security and integrity of data exchanges between robots, ensuring transparency and tamper-proof record keeping.

- **Firewalls and Intrusion Detection:** Deploying firewalls and intrusion detection systems can prevent unauthorized access and monitor network traffic for suspicious activities.

- **Continuous Monitoring:** Regular monitoring of robot communications can detect anomalies, providing early warnings of potential security breaches.

The advent of 5G technology presents new challenges and vulnerabilities for robots. The speed and low latency of 5G can significantly enhance robot-to-robot and robot-to-infrastructure communications, allowing for near real-time data transfer. However, this also means that any breach or attack can propagate through a network at unprecedented speeds, making the detection and response time crucial.

Edge computing introduces another layer to this ecosystem. By processing data closer to the source—in this case, the robot—decisions can be made faster, a critical aspect for autonomous robots in time-sensitive situations. Yet, this decentralized approach opens new attack vectors. If an edge computing node is compromised, it can potentially feed incorrect information to a robot, leading to errors.

In the world of robotics, effective communication goes beyond mere transmission. It is about authenticity, integrity, and security. As we move towards a world intertwined with robots, our commitment to securing communications is a significant responsibility, ensuring a secure coexistence of machines and humankind.

Robots and Privacy: Protecting Personal Information in a Robotic World

"Privacy, like eating and breathing, is one of life's basic requirements."
– Katherine Neville, author

In a 2022 article from the MIT Technology Review, privacy concerns related to iRobot's Roomba robot vacuums were raised. According to the article, development versions of iRobot's Roomba J7 series captured images of household scenes, which were then sent to Scale AI, a startup that contracts workers around the world to label data used to train artificial intelligence. The images included mundane household scenes as well as some intimate ones. These images were posted to online forums by gig workers in Venezuela. iRobot confirmed that these images were captured by its robot vacuums in 2020. However, they stated that all of them came from "special development robots with hardware and software modifications that are not and never were present on iRobot consumer products for purchase." The devices were given to "paid collectors and employees" who signed written agreements acknowledging that they were sending data streams, including video, back to the organization for training purposes. According to iRobot, the devices were labeled with a bright green sticker that read "video recording in progress," and it was up to those paid data collectors to "remove anything they deem sensitive from any space the robot operates in, including children."

The iRobot incident highlights broader ethical considerations surrounding robotic data collection. As robots become more integrated into our personal lives, it is vital to develop regulatory frameworks that ensure data is collected and used responsibly, respecting individual privacy and autonomy.

This case also highlights the potential risks associated with robots and internet-connected devices in general. The importance of robust data privacy measures should not be underestimated. Consumers want technology that offers convenience, efficiency, and enhanced capabilities. That is part of the reason why many people welcome robots into their personal spaces, homes, workplaces, and even their bodies. Yet, every robotics advancement carries with it inherent questions about the privacy of personal information. Who gets to access it? How is it used? Can you trust that your data will not be misused?

Protecting personal information in a robotic world requires collaboration between robotics manufacturers, software developers, and policymakers. It also involves educating consumers about the potential risks associated with using robots and providing them with transparent information about how their data is collected, stored, and used. Consider these different categories of robots and the potential privacy concerns that they introduce:

- **Domestic Robots:** Devices like smart vacuums, personal assistants, and home security robots can collect data about your living spaces, routines, preferences, and your conversations.

- **Healthcare Robots:** Whether a wearable health monitor or a robotic assistant for surgeries, these devices have access to intimate health details, biometrics, and potentially your genetic makeup.

- **Companion and Care Robots:** Especially pertinent for the elderly or those with specific health needs, these robots can gather data about daily routines, physical challenges, and even emotional states.

Most robots are equipped with a selection of cameras, microphones, and sensors that continuously gather data. Without proper regulation or user knowledge, this data could be stored indefinitely, shared, or sold. As with any connected device, robots are vulnerable to cyberattacks. By exploiting these breaches, malicious individuals can gain access to sensitive data, which can result in extortion or exploiting the robot's functionalities for malicious purposes. By analyzing data from our interactions with robots, algorithms can create precise profiles, predicting our behaviors, preferences, and habits. This information, in the hands of advertisers or other third parties, can lead to manipulative strategies or invasive targeted advertising.

Given the international scope of robotics, it is essential to examine existing and prospective legal frameworks governing robotic privacy. This includes analyzing GDPR implications in Europe, the CCPA in California, and other emerging regulations worldwide. Understanding these legalities can guide manufacturers and policymakers in developing compliant and secure robotic systems.

Another important aspect to consider is user awareness and education. Informing consumers about the risks and safeguards related to robotic privacy is paramount. This can be achieved through transparent communication from manufacturers, educational campaigns, and user-friendly resources that demystify complex privacy terms. Educating consumers empowers them to make informed decisions about the robots they integrate into their personal and professional lives.

Beyond the technical and legal aspects, the ethical implications of robotic data collection deserve attention. This involves questioning the moral boundaries of surveillance, consent, and data usage. By incorporating ethical considerations into the design and deployment of robots, manufacturers and developers can uphold a higher standard of responsibility and public trust.

Some measures that can be taken to safeguard personal information in a robotic world include:

- **Transparent Terms:** Manufacturers must provide clear, easily understandable terms of service that detail exactly what data is collected, how it is used, and how long it is stored.

- **Opt-In Data Collection:** Instead of default data collection, users should have the ability to opt into specific data gathering functionalities, giving them control over their information.

- **Data Minimization:** Only collect and store the minimum amount of data necessary for a robot to perform its tasks effectively. This reduces the risk of sensitive information being exposed.

- **End-to-End Encryption:** Personal data stored or transmitted by robots should be encrypted, making it difficult for unauthorized entities to access.

- **Anonymization of Data:** If data needs to be shared for analysis or improvement purposes, it should be anonymized to protect user identity and privacy.

- **Regular Software Updates:** To safeguard against hacks, robotic devices should receive regular security updates and patches.

- **Physical Privacy Features:** For robots with cameras or microphones, physical shutters or mute functions can provide an added layer of privacy when needed.

- **Two-Factor Authentication (2FA):** Implementing 2FA can add an extra layer of security when users are accessing their personal data or controlling the robot remotely.

- **Data Deletion:** Users should have the ability to delete their data from the robot and the manufacturer's servers when they stop using the robot or upon request.

With robotics, the concept of privacy is extremely important. Personal spaces are increasingly being shared with machines that have the potential to record intimate details. But with conscious effort, informed choices, and collaborative actions, you can harness the benefits of robotics without compromising your personal space.

Robotics Futures: Envisioning a Secure and Ethical Future with Robots

"Individual science fiction stories may seem as trivial as ever to the blinder critics and philosophers of today, but the core of science fiction, its essence, has become crucial to our salvation, if we are to be saved at all."
— Isaac Asimov, science fiction writer

As you consider the future of robotics, it is also useful to consider the past. One of the luminaries in the world of science fiction, Isaac Asimov, profoundly impacted our understanding and perception of robots. Asimov's *Robot* series introduced readers to a future where robots were not just soulless machines but entities ingrained into society. These works were stories of advanced machinery and profound observations on human ethics, morals, and our relationship with technology.

Central to Asimov's portrayal of robots were the "Three Laws of Robotics," which are surprisingly relevant even today. The laws are:

• A robot may not injure a human, or, through inaction, allow a human to come to harm.

• A robot must obey the orders given by humans, except where orders would conflict with the 1st law.

• A robot must protect its own existence if such protection does not conflict with the 1st or 2nd law.

As we envisage a future where robots are a part of every aspect of our lives, the ethical and legal challenges are profound and complex. This requires a rethinking of traditional perspectives on rights, ownership, and liability.

In the world of robotics and AI, the concept of "robot rights" emerges as an intriguing topic. While today's robots lack consciousness and are thus not candidates for "rights" in a human or animal sense, the rapid evolution of robotics and AI invites preemptive discussion on the matter. Should robots with advanced AI have a form of legal personhood, like corporations? As robots potentially develop more autonomous and self improving algorithms, society may need to consider frameworks to address their role and status.

The theft or hijacking of a robot is not just a loss of property; it can be a significant security breach or pose threats to human lives. Imagine a scenario where a humanoid robot is commandeered by malicious actors. The ramifications range from privacy, safety, and financial loss. As such incidents become more commonplace, laws will have to evolve to address the culpability and liability of such actions.

Who is at fault when a fully autonomous robot makes a decision that leads to harm? The programmer, the manufacturer, the owner, or the robot itself? As robotics become more sophisticated, attributing liability becomes murkier. Legal systems will need to adapt to the unique challenges posed by robotic autonomy, perhaps creating new categories of legal responsibility that can better fit the complex nature of automated decision-making.

As we protect robots against cyber threats, ethical considerations around surveillance capabilities and data collection by robots must be scrutinized. The balance between security and privacy remains delicate. Enhanced security measures could lead to robots becoming unwitting spies, collecting data on individuals without consent. Legislation around robot data collection, storage, and sharing will become increasingly critical.

Robotics and cybersecurity do not exist in a vacuum. Different nations have varying capabilities and laws, leading to disparities in how robotics is used and secured. There is an ongoing question of "cyber sovereignty," the idea that every country has the right to govern the cyber activities within its own region. Yet, robots and their communications can be international, necessitating a harmonized approach to cybersecurity that transcends borders.

Looking ahead even further, to a time when robots might be your co-worker, caregiver, and even companion, consider these additional safety and security advances:

- **Self-Healing Robots:** Inspired by biological systems, researchers are exploring robots that can autonomously detect, diagnose, and repair any security breaches or anomalies.

- **Behavioral Analytics:** Advanced AI models could monitor a robot's behavior, comparing it to established norms, and raise flags upon detecting deviations, indicative of potential compromise.

- **Decentralized Security Protocols:** Blockchain and decentralized ledgers can provide a transparent and tamper-proof method for robots to validate data and transactions.

The magnified role of robotics in our future society presents unmatched opportunities and unprecedented challenges. The onus is on researchers, policymakers, industries, and consumers to prioritize cybersecurity. Cybersecurity in robotics is not merely a technical issue; it is laden with ethical implications that must be addressed through thoughtful legislation, international cooperation, and ongoing societal dialogue. Through research and innovations, we can create a future where robots amplify human potential, all while operating within a secure and trustworthy framework.

Chapter 5

Internet of Things (IoT): A Connected World and its Cyber Implications

"If it's smart, it's vulnerable."
– Mikko Hyppönen, author and cybersecurity professional

5

The Connected Revolution

"The internet is like alcohol in some sense. It accentuates what you would do anyway. If you want to be loner, you can be more alone, and if you want to connect, it makes easier to connect."
– Esther Dyson, investor and journalist

In 2019, a Milwaukee-based couple suffered a horrifying incident after their smart home setup was hacked by unknown intruders. The couple claimed that hackers took over their smart home by compromising the connected devices. The attacker played disturbing music from the video system, at a high volume, and spoke to them via a camera in the kitchen and changed the room temperature to the maximum setting by exploiting the thermostat. Initially, the couple thought it was a technical glitch and changed their passwords, but the issue continued. They later changed their network ID, after realizing that someone had hacked their Wi-Fi or Nest system.

As of 2024, the Internet of Things (IoT) has permeated our lives, with an estimated 17.08 billion devices connected worldwide. This number is projected to nearly double to 29.42 billion by 2030, highlighting IoT's integral role in reshaping industries and personal lifestyles. From smart appliances in homes to sophisticated sensors in industrial complexes, IoT's ubiquity is a testament to its transformative power. Yet, this vast network also unveils many cybersecurity challenges, requiring professionals to gain a better understanding of IoT's complexities.

How do IoT devices differ from traditional computers? Are they simply computers connected to the internet, or is there more to it? Why do we need a different approach to securing our IoT devices from potential attacks? But before we dive too deep into this fascinating subject, let us start by clarifying the definition of the Internet of Things (IoT).

IoT devices encompass a wide range of physical objects that have been enhanced with sensors, connectivity, and computational capabilities. This enables IoT devices to gather, share, and respond to data. IoT devices are connected to the internet, enabling convenient communication and interaction. These devices are embedded into our daily lives, spanning various sectors such as health care, transportation, manufacturing, smart homes, and smart cities. Common examples of IoT devices include:

- **Smart Thermostats:** These devices enable remote temperature control and energy management, optimizing heating and cooling systems for efficiency.

- **Health Care/Fitness Trackers:** Wearable IoT devices monitor personal health metrics like heart rate, sleep patterns, and physical activity.

- **Smart Appliances:** Refrigerators, washing machines, and other household appliances can communicate with users, adapt settings, and offer maintenance alerts.

- **Industrial Sensors:** IoT sensors in factories monitor equipment performance, predict maintenance needs, and enhance overall productivity.

- **Smart Cities Infrastructure:** Urban areas use IoT to manage traffic, monitor air quality, and optimize municipal services.

- **Agriculture/Smart Farming:** This includes soil and weather sensors that optimize crop growth conditions.

These examples show the remarkable adaptability and potential of IoT devices. They provide data-driven insights and enhance your ability to control and interact with your environment more efficiently.

IoT devices signify a transformative shift in the methods of data collection, processing, and utilization. These devices offer numerous advantages to individuals, organizations, and society.

- **Enhanced Efficiency:** IoT devices are adept at streamlining processes, making them more efficient. In agriculture, for instance, sensors can monitor soil conditions and automatically adjust irrigation, optimizing resource use and crop yields. In manufacturing, IoT-powered predictive maintenance can help reduce downtime by predicting equipment failures before they occur.

- **Improved Convenience:** Smart homes are a prime example of how IoT can make your life more convenient. Devices like smart speakers, thermostats, and lights can be controlled remotely through smartphone apps or voice commands, allowing you to adjust environments and preferences remotely.

- **Data-Driven Insights:** IoT devices generate vast amounts of data. This data can be harnessed to gain valuable insights, whether it is understanding customer behavior in retail, monitoring patient health in health care, or optimizing logistics in supply chain management.

- **Safety and Security:** IoT devices have the potential to enhance safety and security. In smart cities, for instance, connected cameras and sensors can detect unusual activities, such as accidents or break-ins, and alert authorities in real time. Wearables equipped with health monitoring sensors can provide early warnings for potential health issues.

- **Environmental Impact:** IoT devices can help better understand and mitigate environmental challenges. For instance, air quality sensors can provide real-time data on pollution levels, helping cities take corrective measures to improve air quality.

Almost without noticing, IoT devices have permeated our lives, bringing forth significant advantages and opportunities. However, as you enjoy the convenience and efficiency they offer, it is crucial to recognize that this newfound connectivity also comes with a profound impact on cybersecurity.

Smart Devices, Smart Security

"People are trying to be smart; all I am trying to do is not to be idiotic,
but it's harder than most people think."
– Charlie Munger, American investor and ex-vice chairman of
Berkshire Hathaway

In 2016, one of the most prominent IoT security breaches took place. The Mirai botnet specifically targeted IoT devices like routers, cameras, and digital video recorders (DVRs). Exploiting weak default credentials, the malware infected these devices, enabling the attackers to launch massive, Distributed Denial-of-Service (DDoS) attacks. This incident underscores the criticality of having strong, unique passwords for IoT devices, along with manufacturers promptly providing security updates and patches.

Similarly, in 2017, at a North American casino, cybercriminals gained access to the casino's high-roller database through a smart thermometer in the lobby's fish tank. This breach serves as a reminder that seemingly harmless IoT devices can become entry points for hackers. It emphasizes the necessity of implementing comprehensive network security measures that cover all connected devices.

IoT devices are essentially compact computers, complete with input, output, and processing power. However, what adds complexity is their ubiquitous presence and often unknown location and security status. When it comes to securing IoT devices, different scenarios require specific solutions. These scenarios can be categorized into two types.

Protecting IoT Devices from the World

In a business environment, IoT devices are used for various purposes, from office automation to industrial control systems. However, their presence on the network poses security risks. These devices can be accessed by attackers who may exploit vulnerabilities in their firmware or software to gain a foothold on the network.

Protecting the World from IoT Devices

IoT devices can potentially be exploited as mechanisms for attacks, both within and outside your organization. A compromised IoT device can be used to launch attacks on other devices, networks, or services. This could result in significant disruption and even financial loss.

In both scenarios, securing IoT devices is critical. However, the security measures required may vary depending on the type of device and its purpose. Securing Internet of Things (IoT) devices requires a tailored approach that goes beyond the fundamental cybersecurity practices necessary for standard internet-connected computers. This includes employing basic security measures such as strong authentication, secure communication protocols, and regular software updates. The unique characteristics of IoT devices introduce additional layers of complexity.

- **Massive IoT Attack Surface:** The scale of IoT is one of its most daunting aspects. With billions of devices worldwide, a single vulnerability can be exploited across numerous devices, making security management at this scale incredibly challenging. Compounding this issue is the diverse range of IoT devices, which makes a one-size-fits-all security strategy impractical—each has different capabilities, operating environments, and security requirements.

- **Network Place:** IoT devices reside within corporate or private networks, which can be advantageous for potential attackers. They can exploit IoT devices to conduct covert reconnaissance on the network or launch attacks on external targets, disguising their actions.

- **Limited Resources on IoT Devices:** Many IoT devices face resource constraints, such as limited processing power, memory, and battery life, which can hinder the implementation of comprehensive security measures. Additionally, their persistent connectivity presents continuous exposure to cyber threats, unlike traditional computers that can be turned off or disconnected. This is further exacerbated by the physical deployment of IoT devices, often in remote or harsh environments like offshore oil rigs, increasing their vulnerability due to environmental factors and limited connectivity. Despite the limited resources, IoT devices can be hijacked by attackers to create a server farm for cryptocurrency mining.

- **Extended Lifecycles:** IoT devices also typically have extended lifecycles compared to traditional computers, meaning devices installed years ago might now be operating with outdated security. For example, decade-old smart meters would not have been designed with security controls to address present day cybersecurity risks.

- **Complex Integration and Interoperability:** The complexity of integrating and ensuring interoperability among various IoT devices can create additional security gaps, particularly when these components do not share compatible security standards. For example, consider smart lights that need to connect to a smart hub, which needs to connect to a smart assistant speaker.

- **Data Privacy Concerns:** The vast amount of sensitive data collected by IoT devices raises significant data privacy concerns, requiring robust protection against unauthorized access. As IoT expands the attack surface for cybercriminals, each device becomes a potential entry point into networks, posing risks to the entire ecosystem. The IoT landscape's complexity, characterized by different types of devices and protocols, further complicates uniform security standard implementation.

- **Security as an Afterthought:** Many IoT devices are developed with a primary focus on functionality and cost-effectiveness, often neglecting security considerations. This oversight can lead to vulnerabilities that malicious actors may exploit. Regular firmware and software updates are crucial for maintaining security, but IoT devices, especially those in remote settings, may not receive timely updates, leaving them exposed to threats. Default passwords, often generic and easy to guess, come with devices right out of the box. If left unchanged, they provide a low-hanging fruit for cybercriminals.

- **Supply Chain Risks:** Supply chain vulnerabilities also pose a significant risk, as attackers can target components, firmware, or software during manufacturing and distribution, leading to pre-installed malware or backdoors in devices. The potential for IoT devices to be exploited to create botnets for Distributed Denial-of-

Service (DDoS) attacks presents a serious threat to critical services and infrastructure.

Managing IoT cybersecurity risks in a corporate environment involves adopting the following measures:

- **Asset Management:** Effectively managing and monitoring IoT devices requires meticulous tracking and maintaining an up-to-date inventory of all connected devices.

- **Lifecycle Management:** Often overlooked, identifying devices that have reached end-of-life, and decommissioning obsolete devices, is critical for reducing security risks.

- **Supply Chain Security:** Verify the security of components and firmware throughout the supply chain and establish trust with suppliers.

- **Encryption:** Ensure that data transmitted between IoT devices and the cloud is encrypted.

- **Authentication:** Implement strong authentication mechanisms to verify device and user identity.

- **Passwords:** Modify default passwords and opt for strong, unique passwords.

- **Regular Updates and Patch Management:** Establish a process for regularly updating and patching IoT devices to address known vulnerabilities.

- **Monitoring and Anomaly Detection:** Implement continuous monitoring and anomaly detection systems to identify suspicious activity in real time.

- **Network Segmentation:** Isolate IoT devices from critical network segments to limit the potential impact of a breach. Implement strong physical access controls where possible and regularly monitor device behavior. This is especially important if you are unable to implement the previously mentioned security protections.

The world of IoT devices encompasses a wide array of characteristics that set them apart from traditional computers. IoT devices offer undeniable advantages, including heightened efficiency, convenience, and data-driven insights across various domains. However, the rapid expansion of IoT also introduces unique cybersecurity challenges that require attention. By adopting a proactive and security-focused approach, your organization can fully embrace the potential of IoT while mitigating the associated risks.

Standards and Regulation of IoT

"There's no silver bullet solution with cybersecurity;
a layered defense is the only viable defense."
— James Scott, author and co-founder of the Institute for Critical Infrastructure Technology

Adhering to standards and regulations is a vital aspect of securing an IoT environment. These standards, guidelines, and regulations lay the foundation for comprehensive security measures, providing guidance to manufacturers and users. Following these protocols will result in a safer, more reliable IoT ecosystem.

The International Standards Organization (ISO) has been instrumental in defining a multitude of standards, providing a foundation for various industries. ISO has established several key IoT standards, ensuring the security, interoperability, and efficiency of IoT devices and systems across the globe:

- **ISO/IEC 21823-1:2019:** This standard provides an overview of interoperability as it applies to IoT systems and a framework for interoperability for IoT systems. It enables IoT systems to be built so that entities of the IoT system can exchange and use information efficiently.

- **ISO/IEC 21823-4:2022:** This standard focuses on the interoperability of IoT systems, specifically syntactic interoperability. It provides principles for IoT syntactic interoperability, relevant technologies for syntactic interoperability, the overall structure of the proposed approach, the methodology of metamodel-driven information exchange, and information exchange rules.

- **ISO/IEC 27400:** This is a comprehensive standard that provides guidelines on risks, principles, and controls for the security and privacy of Internet of Things (IoT) solutions.

- **ISO/IEC TR 30166:** Applies to general industrial IoT (IIoT) systems and landscapes, outlining characteristics, technical aspects, and functional and non-functional elements of the IIoT structure.

These standards aim to ensure that IoT devices and systems are secure, interoperable, and efficient. However, it is important to note that the specifics of these standards are complex and technical, and this summary only provides a high-level overview. For more detailed information, refer to the standards documents.

Globally, regulations for IoT are constantly evolving to tackle cybersecurity challenges. A few worth mentioning include:

- **EU's Cyber Resilience Act (2024):** The EU's Cyber Resilience Act aims to safeguard consumers and businesses buying or using products or software with a digital component. The Act introduces mandatory cybersecurity requirements for manufacturers and retailers of such products, with this protection extending throughout the product lifecycle.

- **US IoT Cybersecurity Improvement Act (2020):** The US IoT Cybersecurity Improvement Act requires the National Institute of Standards and Technology (NIST) and the Office of Management and Budget (OMB) to take specified steps to increase cybersecurity for Internet of Things (IoT) devices. Subsequently, the NIST Cybersecurity for IoT Program was released and supports the development and application of standards, guidelines, and related tools to improve the cybersecurity of IoT systems, products, connected devices, and the environments in which they are deployed.

- **Japan's IoT security guidelines:** Japan's Ministry of Internal Affairs and Communications has developed comprehensive IoT security guidelines. An international standard aimed at ensuring the safety and security of IoT systems has been published based on the "IoT Security Guidelines" and "IoT Safety/Security Development Guidelines" formulated by Japan.

By adhering to these standards and regulations, organizations can greatly enhance the security of IoT devices and ecosystems, ensuring the protection of data and infrastructure from potential cyber threats.

Smart Cities: The Pinnacle of IoT Implementation

"Smart cities are those which use innovative solutions to improve quality of life and sustainability, through the integration of technology into all aspects of city life."
– Matteo Robiglio, CEO of the Smart City Innovation Lab

Arguably the most powerful example of IoT transforming our societies is smart cities. The concept of smart cities has rapidly evolved over the past decade, reflecting the growing integration of technology into urban infrastructure and services.

Imagine a city seamlessly integrated with technology, where every aspect, from traffic lights to power grids, is intelligently connected and responsive. This is the vision of a smart city that leverages the power of IoT to enhance the lives of its inhabitants.

At the heart of smart city transformations are a network of interconnected IoT devices that gather and exchange data in real time. Unlike home IoT devices, smart city devices are embedded into various aspects of city infrastructure, and act as intelligent sensors, collecting information about traffic patterns, energy usage, pollution levels, and other vital factors.

The data collected by IoT devices is fed into sophisticated analytics systems, enabling city officials to gain deeper insights into the urban landscape. These insights empower them to make informed decisions, optimize resource allocation, improve efficiency, and address challenges proactively.

Smart cities are not just about collecting data; they are about harnessing it to create a more responsive and efficient environment. For example:

- IoT-enabled traffic lights can adjust their timing based on real-time traffic conditions, reducing congestion and improving commute times.

- Smart parking systems can guide drivers to available parking spots, eliminating the frustration of circling aimlessly.

- Smart grids can optimize energy distribution, minimizing waste and ensuring a stable power supply.

- Smart lighting systems can adjust brightness based on ambient lighting, conserving energy while ensuring adequate illumination.

- Smart waste management systems can optimize collection routes, reducing the environmental impact of waste disposal.

Smart cities are not just about technology; they are about creating a more livable, sustainable, and equitable future for all. By leveraging IoT's transformative power, cities are becoming more responsive, efficient, and citizen-centric, transforming the urban experience for the better.

While smart cities promise numerous benefits, they are also particularly attractive targets for cyberattackers. The attractiveness of smart cities to attackers is rooted in their complex and interconnected IoT infrastructure, which offers multiple points of vulnerability. These urban centers, characterized by a network of IoT devices and sensors, collect and manage a wealth of sensitive data and personal information for municipal services.

Smart cities are built around critical digital infrastructure that governs utilities, transportation systems, and emergency services. Any disruption to these crucial systems can lead to widespread and severe consequences, attracting the attention of not just financially motivated criminals but also state-sponsored attackers aiming to cause significant impact. The extensive network of IoT devices exponentially increases the attack surface, with the sheer number of devices providing numerous potential entry points. This abundance of connected devices, if unmanaged or unmonitored, allows attackers to easily identify and exploit vulnerabilities.

In many cases, the eagerness of cities to adopt smart technologies outpaces the development and implementation of robust cybersecurity strategies. This gap in security awareness and preparedness creates a favorable environment for attackers, who can exploit these weaknesses with little risk of detection or resistance. Smart cities symbolize significant economic and political investments by governments and private entities. Attacks on these projects can lead to substantial disruptions, with far-reaching economic and political implications, making them appealing targets for hacktivists and state actors looking to make a statement or exert influence.

Smart cities are highly vulnerable to a diverse range of cyber threats due to valuable data, critical infrastructure, expansive attack surface, limited security awareness, and the potential for significant economic and political consequences. The development and maintenance of smart city infrastructure requires the implementation of robust cybersecurity measures to safeguard against these threats.

Securing smart cities poses some unique challenges as compared to protecting traditional computer networks. The following challenges highlight the distinctive nature of securing urban technology:

- **Diverse Ecosystem:** Smart cities incorporate a wide range of IoT devices, including traffic cameras, environmental sensors, smart grid components, and more. Each device has unique vulnerabilities, and managing its security is complex and requires specialized expertise.

- **Legacy Infrastructure:** Many smart cities incorporate existing legacy infrastructure that may not have been designed with security in mind. Retrofitting these systems with modern cybersecurity measures is a challenging and costly endeavor.

- **Scale and Complexity:** The vast scale and complexity of smart city systems make them difficult to monitor and secure effectively. The sheer number of devices and the intricacies of their interactions require comprehensive cybersecurity solutions.

- **Privacy Concerns:** As smart cities collect vast amounts of data, privacy concerns are paramount. Balancing the need for data collection with the protection of individual's privacy is a delicate and evolving challenge that smart city administrators must address.

- **Interconnectedness:** Smart city systems are deeply interconnected, with data flowing between various components to make real-time decisions. This interconnectivity increases the potential impact of a successful cyberattack, as one compromised system can affect others.

Resource Constraints

Many cities operate with limited budgets and resources for cybersecurity. Securing a smart city requires substantial investments in technology, personnel, and training.

Given the complexity and challenges involved in securing smart cities, a comprehensive approach to cybersecurity is essential. Here are some strategies and best practices:

- **Security by Design:** Implement security at the design phase for all new smart city projects. This includes strong encryption and access control, amongst others.

- **Education and Training:** Invest in cybersecurity education and training for city staff and IT professionals so that they understand the unique challenges and solutions for securing smart cities.

- **Privacy Protection:** Implement strong privacy protection measures to safeguard the personal data collected by smart city systems. Ensure compliance with data protection regulations.

- **Monitoring and Response:** Establish real-time monitoring and rapid incident response capabilities to detect and mitigate cyber threats as they arise.

- **Updates and Patch Management:** Regularly update and patch all IoT devices and systems to address known vulnerabilities and protect against emerging threats.

Smart cities represent the pinnacle of IoT implementations, offering numerous benefits to residents and urban planners. However, their extensive IoT ecosystems and critical role in urban life make them highly attractive targets for cyberattackers. Securing smart cities requires a comprehensive and proactive approach, acknowledging the unique challenges posed by their scale, complexity, and interconnectedness.

Privacy Concerns and Ethical Implications of IoT

"Once you've lost your privacy, you realize you've lost an extremely valuable thing."
— Billy Graham, American clergyman

The proliferation of the Internet of Things (IoT) is transforming our daily lives and revolutionizing the way we interact with technology. The unparalleled convenience and interconnectivity of IoT devices introduces another substantial consequence, which is the erosion of privacy and the emergence of numerous ethical quandaries. The privacy concerns and ethical implications surrounding IoT devices are complex and therefore demand special consideration.

Ubiquitous Data Collection: A Double-Edged Sword

IoT devices, by their very nature, are prolific data gatherers, often without the explicit knowledge or consent of the users.

In 2018, Strava, a fitness-tracking app, inadvertently exposed the locations of secret military bases worldwide. This happened when Strava published a global heatmap that revealed the exercise routes of its users. The heatmap was detailed enough to give away location data about military personnel on active service. In locations like Afghanistan, Djibouti, and Syria, the users of Strava seemed to be almost exclusively foreign military personnel, meaning that bases stood out brightly.

For instance, in Helmand province, Afghanistan, the locations of forward operating bases could be clearly seen, glowing white against the black map. The base itself was not visible on the satellite views of commercial providers such as Google Maps or Apple Maps, yet it could be seen through Strava.

The Strava example underscores the need for robust data privacy, where user consent, transparency, and data minimization are not just best practices but mandatory standards. Ensuring that users are well-informed about the data being collected and its intended use is crucial in maintaining trust and integrity in IoT ecosystems.

Data Ownership and Sharing: Demystifying the Complex Web

Data ownership and data sharing within the IoT ecosystem add another layer of complexity to privacy concerns. Users often remain oblivious to the extent to which their data is shared with third parties, including advertisers, data brokers, and other stakeholders. This lack of transparency around data ownership and sharing practices creates a lack of trust between users and IoT service providers. Additionally, the potential misuse of shared data raises ethical questions about the responsible handling of sensitive information. One very important aspect to consider is the fact that the data your IoT devices process might not have significant privacy implications, but it can be correlated with other publicly available information to create serious privacy risks for your customers.

The Amazon-owned organization, Ring, has had two separate security incidents. In one incident, user data was accidentally revealed to both Facebook and Google via third-party trackers embedded into their Android application. In another incident, cybercriminals successfully hacked into several connected doorbells and home monitoring systems.

Hackers were able to access live feeds from the cameras around customers' homes and communicate remotely using the devices' integrated microphones and speakers. Subsequently, in May 2023, the Federal Trade Commission charged Ring with compromising its customers' privacy by allowing any employee or contractor to access consumers' private videos and by failing to implement basic privacy and security protections.

The cases of Strava and Ring illustrate the significant risks associated with data collection, ownership, and sharing in IoT ecosystems. This requires robust data governance, transparency in data collection and sharing practices, and stringent security measures to protect sensitive user information. The IoT landscape, with its profound potential for innovation, must navigate these challenges thoughtfully and responsibly to maintain user trust.

Balancing Surveillance and Privacy: An Ethical Tightrope

The deployment of IoT devices for surveillance purposes raises significant ethical concerns, especially in public spaces. While these devices can enhance security measures, they also have the potential to infringe upon individuals' right to privacy. Unauthorized surveillance, including the monitoring of private conversations or tracking of movements without consent, can lead to an Orwellian society where personal freedoms are curtailed, and individual autonomy is compromised.

For example, consider the widespread use of surveillance in China. The Chinese government has implemented a social credit system that uses surveillance technologies, such as facial recognition, to monitor and track citizens' behavior, ultimately affecting their access to certain services and freedoms. The extent of the surveillance system is difficult to grasp, with cities like Chongqing boasting 2.58 million surveillance cameras in 2019. This surveillance extends online to the internet giants like Alibaba and Tencent sharing troves of behavioral data with the government. Citizens' behavior is monitored and scrutinized, and they are given scores and ranked according to rules set by the government. "Model" citizens enjoy perks such as reduced bus fares, but those with low scores lose certain rights and are blacklisted.

Chinese technology companies have made state-of-the-art surveillance systems affordable and accessible, leading to the spread of state surveillance globally. Specifically, more than 140 cities around the world, including Kuala Lumpur, Nairobi, and Quito, are being transformed into Chinese-enhanced "safe cities" and "smart cities."

This overreaching use of IoT devices for surveillance purposes further highlights the need for ethical considerations in the development and deployment of these devices. This is a significant risk whether you are a producer or a consumer of IoT devices, especially considering the insecure nature of some IoT solutions. Incorrect handling of IoT devices can expose your organization to significant risk.

For another example, in 2019, Airbnb, the popular online marketplace for lodging, faced privacy concerns when several customers reported finding hidden cameras in their rental properties. These hidden cameras, which were connected to the internet, were recording guests without their knowledge or consent. In response to these incidents, Airbnb has implemented strict policies regarding the use of security devices in their listings.

Ethical Dilemmas in Data Usage

The ethical implications of IoT data usage are profound. The commodification of personal data for targeted advertising or other commercial purposes raises questions about the ethical boundaries of data exploitation. The potential for discriminatory practices based on data analytics further accentuates the ethical dilemmas, perpetuating biases and reinforcing societal inequalities. For a chilling example of what can go wrong, consider what happened to Robert Williams. In 2020, he was wrongfully arrested after an incorrect facial recognition match led to his arrest. Detroit police had matched grainy surveillance footage of a crime to Williams' driver's license photo using a facial recognition service.

The development and implementation of IoT devices requires the establishment of robust guiding principles for privacy and ethics in IoT. These principles are pivotal in upholding the integrity of IoT technology and promoting its responsible usage. They are as follows:

- **Adherence to Data Protection Regulations:** It is imperative to strictly comply with data protection laws. Incorporating regular privacy impact assessments into IoT projects is essential.

- **Establishment of a Data Governance Framework:** A comprehensive data governance framework needs to be established. This framework should emphasize the importance of informed consent, provide clear guidelines on data collection, and outline explicit usage policies.

- **Promotion of Ethical Data Handling:** Ethical data handling practices should be encouraged. This can be achieved by adhering to the principles of data minimization and purpose limitation, and by ensuring the accuracy of the data collected.

The advent of IoT has significantly expanded the boundaries of technological innovation, but it has also amplified privacy concerns and raised complex ethical questions. Striking a balance between technological advancement and safeguarding individual privacy demands a comprehensive reassessment of regulatory frameworks, industry standards, and consumer awareness.

The Future of IoT: Opportunities and Predictions

"The future is already here; it's just not evenly distributed."
– William Gibson, American speculative fiction author,
who coined the term "cyberspace" in 1982

As the Internet of Things (IoT) continues its expansive integration into various facets of life, from smart homes to industrial automation, the global landscape of IoT regulation is evolving. This advancement underscores the urgency for harmonizing IoT security standards worldwide. While significant, these objectives face complexities due to differing priorities and legal frameworks among nations, making international cooperation and dialogue essential, albeit challenging.

The future of IoT is marked by its impact on daily life, promising to transform multiple domains. In homes, interconnected devices will intelligently manage living environments, enhancing energy efficiency, and convenience. Industries will see IoT-driven enhancements in processes and maintenance, leading to greater productivity and reduced operational costs. Similarly, the emergence of smart cities will herald a new era of sustainable urban living, with integrated infrastructure and public services.

Beyond these familiar areas, IoT's application in agriculture, sustainability, and health care is poised for exciting developments. In agriculture, IoT's role in monitoring and optimizing conditions will revolutionize farming practices, leading to sustainable resource use and increased yields. The sustainability sector will benefit from IoT-enabled smart energy systems, contributing significantly to carbon emission reduction. In health care, IoT wearables will transform patient care through real-time monitoring and data-driven insights, enhancing preventive health strategies.

However, as IoT technologies advance, their convergence with other emerging technologies such as AI, blockchain, 5G, edge computing, and advanced materials like graphene sensors will present new benefits and challenges. This convergence will redefine the cybersecurity landscape, with AI enhancing threat detection, and blockchain providing a secure framework for data integrity and control. The integration of these technologies into IoT systems promises enhanced security but also poses novel vulnerabilities and ethical considerations, especially in areas like health care and public surveillance.

The future of IoT, while rich with innovation, calls for a sustained focus on cybersecurity, privacy, and ethical considerations. It is crucial for manufacturers, policymakers, and users to collaborate in fostering a cybersecurity-aware culture and advocate for secure IoT practices. By championing principles of "security-by-design" and "privacy-by-design," and striving for a balanced regulatory framework, the potential of IoT can be fully realized in a manner that is safe, efficient, and respectful of privacy and ethical standards.

Chapter 6

Autonomous Vehicles:
Securing the Future of Transportation

"Fasten your seatbelts. It's going to be a bumpy night."
– Margo Channing (Bette Davis) in *All about Eve*

6

Exploring Autonomous Vehicles: More than Just Self-Driving Cars

"Self-driving cars are the natural extension of active safety and obviously something we should do."
— Elon Musk, Tesla and SpaceX CEO

At the 1939 World's Fair in New York City, General Motors, an automotive manufacturing organization, presented a model electric vehicle that was guided by radio-controlled electromagnetic fields. This was not just any vehicle but a concept of a self-driving car that was far ahead of its time.

Fast forward to the 1980s when the first self-sufficient and truly autonomous vehicles began to appear. In 1984, Carnegie Mellon University's Navlab and ALV projects were significant milestones in the field of autonomous vehicles. The Navlab project was initiated by the Robotics Institute at Carnegie Mellon University (CMU) with the mission of using computer vision to create autonomous navigation. It was part of the Autonomous Land Vehicle (ALV) program funded by the U.S. Department of Defense's Advanced Research Projects Agency (ARPA).

The project led to the development of a series of robot cars, vans, SUVs, and buses. The Navlab project's first venture into the outdoor environment with a robot was the Terragator. From 1984 to 1992, the Terragator served as a testbed machine for coming innovations.

Then, in 1987, the Eureka Prometheus Project (PROgraMme for a European Traffic of Highest Efficiency and Unprecedented Safety), a collaboration between Mercedes-Benz and Bundeswehr University Munich, was the largest R&D project ever in the field of driverless cars. It received €749,000,000 in funding from the EUREKA member states. The project culminated in 1994, when their twin robot vehicles, VaMP and VITA-2, drove more than 1,000 kilometers on a Paris multi-lane highway in standard heavy traffic, at speeds up to 130 km/h. They demonstrated autonomous driving in free lanes, convoy driving, automatic tracking of other vehicles, and lane changes, left and right, with autonomous passing of other cars.

But the story of autonomous vehicles is not confined to the roads of our cities. It extends beyond Earth to Mars. In the early 1990s, NASA developed the Mars rover Sojourner, an autonomous device capable of intelligently sensing, identifying, classifying, and navigating through specific obstacles. In July 1997, Sojourner landed on Mars, marking a significant milestone in the history of autonomous vehicles. It was the first time NASA scientists used a small, wheeled robot to study the surface of Mars. The rover was only about the size of a microwave oven, but it shared lots of important new information with scientists. Sojourner was operational on Mars for 92 Martian days (95 Earth days). It traveled just over 100 meters (330 ft) by the time communication was lost. The last signal from the rover was received on the morning of October 7, 1997.

The Sojourner rover was the forerunner of the more advanced Spirit, Opportunity, and Curiosity rovers. This first rover demonstrated key technologies and built technical competencies needed for designing and operating the later generations of wheeled Martian explorers. NASA's Opportunity rover set the record for the longest operational lifespan for a Mars rover, at 14 years and 136 days. Opportunity landed on Mars on 25 January 2004, and transitioned into a low-power sleep mode during a planet-wide dust storm on 10 June 2018. Despite attempts to reestablish contact, NASA officially declared the Opportunity mission complete on February 13, 2019. During its mission, Opportunity traveled more than the distance of a marathon (26.2 miles, or 42.1 kilometers) on Mars. Its odometer read 28.06 miles (45.16 km) at the time of its last contact.

These early developments laid the foundation for the autonomous vehicles that we see today. Autonomous vehicles (AVs) are one of the most thrilling emerging technologies, poised to continue to revolutionize transportation and urban infrastructure.

But what are autonomous vehicles (AVs) exactly? AVs are vehicles that are equipped with advanced sensors, artificial intelligence, and other technologies to navigate and operate without human intervention. They are designed to perceive their surroundings, identify obstacles, make decisions, and self-navigate, all without a human driver. The degree of autonomy can vary, with some vehicles requiring occasional human input and others being entirely autonomous. Examples of autonomous vehicles include the following major categories:

- **Autonomous Cars:** Passenger vehicles with technology to navigate autonomously, avoiding road hazards and responding to traffic conditions.

- **Autonomous Trucks:** Developed for long-haul transportation and delivery services.

- **Autonomous Buses and Shuttles:** Used in controlled environments like university campuses, airports, and specific city districts.

- **Autonomous Trains:** Employed in various metro systems globally.

- **Drones:** Deployed for commercial purposes such as package delivery, medical supply transport, and critical infrastructure inspection.

- **Electric vertical take-off and landing vehicles (eVTOLs):** Small aircraft for urban air mobility, personal transportation, and cargo delivery, capable of vertical takeoff and horizontal flight.

- **Autonomous Ships and Ferries:** Developed for cargo and passenger transportation.

- **Space Rovers:** Designed for extraterrestrial exploration, equipped with advanced navigation and data-gathering technologies.

- **Space Rockets:** Integrated with autonomous technologies for space exploration and travel, capable of navigating to specific destinations and returning safely to Earth.

- **Satellites:** Orbit Earth autonomously, performing tasks like weather monitoring, GPS navigation, scientific research, and communications, equipped with computers and sensors for autonomous operation and course adjustment.

It is worth noting that the level of autonomy can vary across different models and types of vehicles. Some may require human intervention in certain scenarios, while others can operate completely autonomously under specific conditions.

- **Technological Foundations and Innovations:** Autonomous vehicles leverage a multitude of onboard sensing and localization technologies, including lidar, radar, cameras, global navigation satellite system (GNSS), and map data. Coupled with AI-driven decision-making, these technologies enable vehicles to operate with limited or no human supervision or intervention. The foundation of autonomous vehicles lies in the seamless integration of cutting-edge technologies, each playing a vital role in enhancing their functionality and ensuring safety.

- **Sensory Perception Technologies:** Central to the operation of autonomous vehicles are sensory technologies such as radar, light detection and ranging (LiDAR), and optical cameras. These systems work collaboratively to provide a comprehensive, real-time understanding of the vehicle's surroundings, essential for navigation and obstacle avoidance.

- **Computer Vision:** This technology allows vehicles to interpret and make sense of visual information, mimicking human visual perception. It plays a vital role in recognizing traffic signals, road signs, and other important visual cues.

- **Advanced Control Systems:** Control systems involve the use of control algorithms to design switch control strategies combining accelerator and brake. A fuzzy control algorithm based on vehicle tracking and trajectory deviation is designed to enhance the vehicle's stability during steering.

- **Artificial Intelligence (AI):** AI algorithms are the driving force behind the decision-making capabilities of autonomous vehicles. These algorithms process data from sensory inputs, enabling the vehicle to learn from diverse driving conditions and make informed decisions.

- **Global Positioning Systems (GPS), Navigation, and Mapping:** High-precision GPS systems are crucial for accurate positioning and route planning, offering essential guidance to autonomous vehicles.

  High-definition (HD) maps are crucial for autonomous driving, allowing a driverless vehicle to localize itself with high precision, mapping its exact location with respect to the surrounding environment. As opposed to traditional maps, HD maps for self-driving cars are not intended for general navigation. HD maps for autonomous driving integrate and analyze sets of data from multiple sources, such as vehicle sensors, LiDAR, onboard cameras, satellite imagery, and GPS in real time.

- **Connectivity (V2X Communication):** Vehicle-to-everything (V2X) communication is a critical enabler for autonomous vehicles, referring to the car's communication system, where information from sensors and other sources travels via high-bandwidth, low-latency, high-reliability links. There are several components of V2X, including vehicle-to-vehicle (V2V), vehicle-to-infrastructure (V2I), vehicle-topedestrian (V2P), and vehicle-to-network (V2N) communications. In this environment, cars will talk to other cars, to infrastructure such as traffic lights or parking spaces, to smartphone-toting pedestrians, and to data centers via cellular networks.

- **Securing Autonomous Vehicles:** As autonomous vehicles become more sophisticated and increasingly integrated into our daily lives, securing these technologies becomes essential. AVs rely on complex interconnected systems, all of which are vulnerable to cyberattacks. Recent stories highlight the urgent need for robust cybersecurity measures.

In 2021, a group of researchers successfully hacked a Tesla Model Y's autopilot system. While they conducted the attack in a controlled environment, it underscored the potential risks to autonomous vehicle systems. Vulnerabilities could be exploited by malicious actors to compromise safety and privacy.

In 2022, Daimler, one of the world's leading truck manufacturers, faced a major cybersecurity breach. The incident raised concerns about the security of autonomous trucking systems, as hackers gained unauthorized access to critical vehicle functions.

These stories emphasize that securing autonomous vehicles is critical. It is essential to develop technologies following security by design principles, which focuses on implementing comprehensive security measures at every stage of the autonomous vehicle development lifecycle.

Securing autonomous vehicles goes beyond traditional cybersecurity practices. It involves safeguarding not only the vehicle's digital components but also the physical safety of passengers and pedestrians.

- **Security by Design:** Cybersecurity should be an integral part of the design and development process for autonomous vehicles. This principle involves identifying potential threats and vulnerabilities from the outset and implementing robust security measures throughout the entire product lifecycle.

- **Secure Communication Protocols:** Autonomous vehicles rely on constant communication with other vehicles, infrastructure, and central control systems. Ensuring the confidentiality and integrity of these communications is crucial to prevent unauthorized access and data tampering.

- **Robust Authentication:** Implementing strong authentication mechanisms is vital to verify the legitimacy of commands and data exchanged between autonomous vehicles and their control systems. It is key to analyze the storage of authentication credentials in and outside the vehicle and strictly limit who can access stored credentials.

- **Regular Software Updates:** Autonomous vehicles require frequent software updates to patch vulnerabilities and improve performance. Vehicle makers must establish secure update mechanisms to prevent malicious actors from exploiting update processes. The updates must also be easy to install (ideally without user intervention), to avoid creating a significant army of *zombie* vehicles that are running old, outdated, and vulnerable software.

- **Behavioral Anomaly Detection:** Employing AI and machine learning algorithms to detect abnormal vehicle behavior can help identify potential cyberattacks or system malfunctions in real time, allowing for immediate responses. Behavior analysis is key to prevent advanced attacks from affecting your vehicles and your business.

- **Physical Security:** Protecting the physical components of autonomous vehicles, such as sensors and control units, is essential. Tamper-evident hardware and secure storage solutions can mitigate the risk of physical attacks. This is particularly important for components that host your most delicate information, such as authentication credentials, critical vehicle information, or IP-protected business data.

In addition to cybersecurity, the significance of public perception and acceptance should not be underestimated when it comes to technological advancements. How often have we encountered individuals expressing doubts and concerns regarding the safety of autonomous vehicles? This societal skepticism and apprehension towards autonomous technologies is not a new phenomenon.

In the late 19th century, elevators were manually operated by skilled attendants. Passengers relied on these operators not just for movement between floors but for safety and assurance. The concept of stepping into an elevator without a human operator was, at the time, unthinkable. The transition to automated elevators in the early 20th century was met with skepticism and apprehension. People were hesitant to trust their lives to a seemingly impersonal machine.

However, as technology advanced, so did public confidence. What was initially a source of anxiety, gradually became accepted and eventually expected. The key to this acceptance was a gradual introduction coupled with proven safety records. This shift was not just technological but psychological, as society adapted to and eventually embraced the new norm.

Today, the autonomous vehicle industry is at a similar juncture. Industry professionals are witnessing a gradual but significant shift in public perception. Initially, self-driving cars were met with a mix of curiosity and concern. The idea of ceding control to an AI system was daunting for many, echoing the apprehension once felt towards unmanned elevators.

Waymo's driverless cars have surpassed 7 million miles, including more than 4 million in San Francisco since the start of 2023. Over this distance, Waymo vehicles had three crashes with injuries. All three injuries were minor. If those same miles had been driven by typical human drivers in the same cities, 13 injury crashes would be expected. A study released by Waymo shows that its robotaxis have a 90% lower crash rate than human drivers in San Francisco.

Just as with elevators, exposure and education are playing pivotal roles in transforming public opinion. Testimonials from early adopters, demonstrations of safety features, and transparency about the technology have been instrumental in building trust. The narrative around autonomous vehicles is shifting from a focus on novelty to an emphasis on their potential benefits, such as increased safety, reduced traffic congestion, and enhanced mobility for the elderly and disabled.

Globally, the acceptance of autonomous vehicles varies, influenced by cultural, regulatory, and infrastructural factors. In regions with strong technological infrastructure and supportive regulatory environments, there is more rapid integration and acceptance. Conversely, in regions where technology adoption is slower and regulatory frameworks are less supportive, skepticism persists.

Nevertheless, the global trajectory mirrors the path of the automated elevator, where an initial hesitation gives way to gradual acceptance and integration into daily life.

The story of the elevator serves as a compelling parallel to the journey of autonomous vehicles. It reminds industry professionals that public acceptance is a process that requires time, education, and a demonstration of safety and benefits. As autonomous vehicles continue to evolve and demonstrate their value, we can anticipate a future where they are as ubiquitous and accepted as the automated elevators of our buildings, a once novel technology that became an indispensable part of modern life.

As these vehicles become increasingly integrated into our lives, we must consider their broader impact. From safety and accessibility to environmental benefits and economic transformation, autonomous vehicles have the power to shape our future in countless ways.

Securing the Highways: Cybersecurity Challenges in Autonomous Cars and Trucks

"What kind of insurance ought a self-driving car to have?
If it goes wrong, who's liable?"
— Margareta Drzeniek-Hanouz, head of Economic Progress Initiative,
World Economic Forum

Having gained a broad understanding of autonomous vehicles and the associated societal and cybersecurity challenges, let us now narrow our focus to autonomous cars and trucks. These are often referred to as self-driving or driverless vehicles. They are designed to be fully capable of navigating streets and highways, making informed decisions without any human input.

Imagine a day when you effortlessly glide past a car or truck, only to realize there is no one behind the wheel. Yikes! It is an experience most of us have yet to encounter, but one that is likely to become a reality sooner than we might expect.

These vehicles rely on a combination of advanced technologies, including sensors, artificial intelligence, machine learning, and GPS navigation, to perceive their surroundings, understand traffic rules, and execute complex driving maneuvers. Autonomous cars aim to revolutionize personal transportation by enhancing safety and convenience, while autonomous trucks will transform the logistics and freight industries by improving efficiency and reducing costs. With the increasing frequency and complexity of cyberattacks, it is crucial to prioritize the security of vehicles. This section will examine the distinct cybersecurity challenges posed by autonomous cars and trucks, as well as explore potential strategies to mitigate these risks.

- **AI Attacks:** Attacks on AI can pose a significant threat to autonomous cars and trucks by exploiting their reliance on artificial intelligence and machine learning algorithms. Malicious actors could manipulate the input data received by sensors, causing the AI systems to misinterpret the environment, potentially leading to dangerous decisions. Additionally, adversarial attacks, which involve injecting subtle, specially crafted inputs, could deceive AI systems into making erroneous judgments, such as misidentifying traffic signs or obstacles. In 2017, researchers showed that altering road signs can confuse self-driving cars. For instance, researchers from Tencent demonstrated that by adding stickers to road signs, they could cause a self-driving car to misinterpret the sign. In another study, researchers showed that a Tesla self-driving car could be fooled by black tape on a road sign, leading to dangerous acceleration.

  If the AI models used in autonomous vehicles are not adequately protected, they may be susceptible to model poisoning attacks, where attackers insert malicious data during the training process, compromising the vehicle's decision-making capabilities. As AI continues to play a pivotal role in autonomous vehicle technology, ensuring its resilience to attacks becomes paramount in safeguarding the safety and security of these vehicles on our roads.

- **Vulnerable Communication Networks:** One of the primary challenges in securing autonomous cars and trucks lies in the communication networks they rely on. These vehicles constantly exchange data with other vehicles, infrastructure, and the cloud, forming the foundation of their decision-making process. Recent stories have highlighted the vulnerabilities in these networks. For instance, in 2021, a team of researchers successfully hacked into a Tesla Model X's autopilot system using a drone-mounted hacking device. This incident underscored the need for robust encryption and authentication mechanisms to safeguard the communication between autonomous vehicles and external systems.

- **Remote Exploitation:** The ability to remotely exploit autonomous cars and trucks presents significant cybersecurity concerns. Recent stories have depicted scenarios where malicious actors gain unauthorized access to vehicle systems.

In 2015, security researchers successfully hacked a Jeep Cherokee's infotainment system, gaining control over critical functions, including the brakes and steering. In 2022, a security researcher demonstrated the remote takeover of a Tesla Model 3, highlighting the potential consequences of such breaches.

Remote exploitation can lead to dangerous situations, ranging from vehicle theft to causing accidents by manipulating the vehicle's behavior. Addressing this challenge requires the implementation of strict logical access controls and continuous monitoring of vehicle software.

- **Software Vulnerabilities:** Autonomous cars and trucks are driven by complex software systems, making them susceptible to software vulnerabilities. Recent stories have shown how these vulnerabilities can be exploited. For example, in 2020, a critical vulnerability in the software of a major manufacturer was discovered. This vulnerability could have allowed attackers to take control of the vehicle's steering and acceleration. To overcome this challenge, manufacturers must embrace stringent software development practices, such as comprehensive code reviews and penetration testing. Additionally, manufacturers must implement robust vulnerability management and patch management solutions to promptly address any identified vulnerabilities.

- **Data Privacy Concerns:** The vast amount of data generated and processed by autonomous cars and trucks raises significant data privacy concerns. Recent stories have shed light on the potential misuse of this data. In 2021, it was revealed that some autonomous car manufacturers were collecting extensive data on passenger activities and locations without their knowledge or consent. In November 2022, Waymo, a pioneer in AV technology, launched a fully autonomous ride-hailing service in Phoenix, Arizona. Although successful, the vast amounts of passenger data collected were concerning.

  Protecting data privacy in an autonomous car ecosystem requires robust data anonymization, encryption, and transparent data usage policies. In certain countries or regions, such as the European Union (EU), it is crucial to provide readily accessible options for obtaining explicit consent and exercising the right to opt out.

- **Supply Chain Vulnerabilities:** The supply chain for components is extensive and global, making it vulnerable to cyberattacks. Recent stories have exposed supply chain vulnerabilities in various industries. In 2022, a major semiconductor manufacturer experienced a supply chain attack that impacted the automotive sector, disrupting the production of components. Securing the supply chain requires strict scrutiny of suppliers, third-party audits, and diversification of component sources to mitigate risks. Several manufacturers have increased their in-house development and production of components.

- **Human-Machine Interaction:** While autonomous cars and trucks are designed to reduce the need for human intervention, they still require interaction with passengers and operators. Recent stories have highlighted the risks associated with human-machine interaction. In 2023, a fatal accident occurred when a passenger misinterpreted the vehicle's capabilities and failed to take control in a critical situation. Ensuring safe and effective human-machine interaction is crucial, requiring clear communication of system limitations and continuous user education.

- **Regulations:** Many countries have started government-level discourse around autonomous vehicles. These include Australia, Canada, China, Germany, New Zealand, the United Kingdom, and the United States. The United States leads the way on technology and innovation, with more than 50% of cities currently preparing their streets for self-driving vehicles. More than 50 countries, including Japan, South Korea, and the EU member states, have agreed on common regulations for vehicles that can take over some driving functions.

The UK government has introduced the Automated Vehicles Bill (2023). This bill sets the legal framework for the safe deployment of self-driving vehicles in Great Britain. It implements the recommendations of a 4-year review of regulation for self-driving vehicles carried out by the Law Commission of England and Wales and the Scottish Law Commission. The bill aims to instill confidence in the autonomous vehicle industry by setting explicit regulations concerning liability in the event of crashes.

The European Commission has published a set of rules that automated driving systems (ADS) must meet to be approved. The revised General Safety Regulation applies from 6 July 2022 and establishes the legal framework for the approval of driverless and automated vehicles in the EU. The rules will first apply to new vehicle types from 7 July 2024. The Commission's Sustainable and Smart Mobility Strategy specifies that by 2030, automated mobility will be deployed on a large scale across the EU.

The cybersecurity challenges in autonomous cars and trucks are multifaceted and evolving, requiring constant vigilance and innovation. Some of the featured stories provide real-world examples of the threats and vulnerabilities that autonomous cars and trucks face, emphasizing the urgency of addressing these issues. They also represent ongoing research and development efforts to enhance the security and reliability of this technology. To secure the future of transportation, stakeholders, including manufacturers, regulatory bodies, and cybersecurity experts, must collaborate to develop and implement robust security standards and measures. This includes securing communication networks, preventing remote exploitation, addressing software vulnerabilities, safeguarding data privacy, securing the supply chain, and improving human-machine interaction.

Unmanned Voyages: Cybersecurity in Autonomous Boats and Submersibles

"A ship in port is safe, but that's not what ships are built for."
— Grace Hopper, computer programmer

Autonomous naval vessels, including boats and submersibles, are becoming increasingly prevalent in the maritime industry. Autonomous naval vessels refer to boats and submersibles that are designed to operate in aquatic environments without the need for human control. These vessels leverage advanced navigation, communication, and data processing technologies to perform various tasks independently. The degree of autonomy can vary, ranging from remotely controlled systems to fully autonomous ones where the vessels are capable of self-navigation, decision-making, and problem-solving. While autonomous boats operate on the water's surface, autonomous submersibles function underwater, often used for deep-sea exploration, scientific research, surveillance, and resource extraction.

In 2017, a project known as Roboat was launched as an autonomous, electric boat designed to navigate the busy canals of Amsterdam. The project was a collaboration between the Massachusetts Institute of Technology (MIT) and the Amsterdam Institute for Advanced Metropolitan Solutions (AMS Institute). The Roboat has several use cases, including passenger transport, logistics (waste collection), and surveying water infrastructure and monitoring water quality. It is equipped with sensors, lasers, navigation systems, and cameras, which allow it to scan the canals, avoid obstacles, and determine the ideal route. The boat is self-learning and adapts its abilities based on experiences on the water.

Autonomous naval vessels are unique compared to other autonomous vehicles, primarily due to their operation within a complex and dynamic marine environment. Unlike land-based vehicles, these vessels must navigate a three-dimensional space, accommodating variables such as currents, tides, and wind while also dealing with other moving objects like ships, marine life, and debris. The communication systems of these vessels must be robust enough to function effectively under challenging conditions, like underwater where radio signals are severely limited. Consequently, they often use acoustic communications, which come with their own set of challenges, such as lower data rates and higher latency. The isolation and vastness of the maritime environment requires these vehicles to have a high degree of self-sufficiency, with the ability to perform long-duration missions and handle unforeseen situations without immediate human intervention.

Autonomous maritime vessels have been employed in a variety of sectors and for a multitude of purposes.

Key examples of their applications include:

- **Deep-Sea Exploration:** Autonomous submersibles are frequently used in deep-sea exploration, where they can reach depths difficult or impossible for manned vessels to survive. These submersibles can capture high-resolution images and gather data about the ocean floor, marine life, and underwater geological formations, contributing significantly to oceanographic research.

- **Fisheries Research:** Autonomous ships can track fish populations and migration patterns over extended periods. This data helps scientists understand the health of marine ecosystems and aids in the management of fisheries.

- **Surveillance and Defense:** Autonomous boats and submersibles can carry out surveillance missions without endangering human lives. They are used in military operations for tasks such as mine detection, reconnaissance, and tracking enemy vessels, providing crucial strategic advantages.

- **Oil and Gas Industry:** Autonomous underwater vehicles (AUVs) are used extensively to improve operational efficiency and safety, by mapping seabeds, pipeline inspection, and detection of leaks.

- **Search and Rescue Operations:** Autonomous boats can be deployed in search and rescue missions, using thermal imaging and sonar to locate individuals lost at sea.

- **Climate Research:** Autonomous vessels can gather crucial meteorological and oceanographic data, contributing to the understanding of climate change and its impact on the oceans.

These applications underscore the potential of autonomous naval vessels to revolutionize maritime industries and contribute significantly to scientific research. As technology continues to evolve, we can expect further advancements and innovative uses for these autonomous systems.

Unmanned vessels present a wide range of advantages, such as improved efficiency and decreased human error. However, they also introduce distinctive cybersecurity challenges that must not be overlooked. In this section, we will explore the specific cybersecurity threats posed by autonomous naval vessels, supported by anecdotes that underscore the seriousness of these issues.

- **Vulnerabilities in Communication Systems:** Autonomous naval vessels heavily rely on robust communication systems to operate effectively. They communicate with central control stations, other vessels, and various sensors through wireless networks. However, these communication channels are susceptible to cyberattacks with the potential for malicious actors to disrupt the operations of autonomous boats and submersibles, possibly leading to disastrous consequences.

  To address this challenge, the cybersecurity of communication systems for autonomous naval vessels must be fortified with robust encryption, intrusion detection systems, and continuous monitoring to detect and respond to any suspicious activities.

- **Remote Hijacking Threats:** The concept of remotely hijacking autonomous boats and submersibles may appear as if it is straight out of a science fiction film, but it is a genuine and pressing concern. Weaknesses in onboard software and control systems may enable hackers to seize control of these vessels from a distance, potentially causing them to deviate from their intended course.

  To mitigate remote hijacking threats, manufacturers and operators must invest in robust cybersecurity practices, including regular software updates, penetration testing, and the implementation of strict access controls to prevent unauthorized access to the vessel's control systems.

- **Sensor Manipulation**: The sensors used in autonomous naval vessels play a crucial role in navigation, collision avoidance, and data collection. Cyberattacks that manipulate or disable these sensors can have dire consequences.

  To counter sensor manipulation threats, sensor data integrity must be maintained through secure authentication and encryption mechanisms. Additionally, redundancy in sensor systems and the ability to detect anomalies in sensor data can help identify and mitigate attacks in real time.

- **Supply Chain Vulnerabilities**: The supply chain for autonomous naval vessels is complex, involving numerous components and software from different vendors. This complexity can introduce vulnerabilities if any of the components or software contains flaws or backdoors.

  To address supply chain vulnerabilities, organizations must conduct thorough security assessments of all components and software used in autonomous naval vessels, establish secure procurement practices, and maintain strict control over the supply chain to prevent the introduction of compromised elements.

- **GPS Spoofing and Jamming:** GPS spoofing and jamming attacks can mislead autonomous vessels by providing false location information or disrupting GPS signals, potentially causing navigation errors. Attacks can manipulate GPS signals to steer the vessel into running aground or steer the vessel into an area of the attacker's control. This type of attack is particularly relevant when large fleets exist that are self-steering and there is little to no monitoring in place.

To mitigate GPS spoofing and jamming risks in autonomous vessels, a multi-layered approach should be employed. This includes integrating multi-factor localization technologies like radar and LiDAR alongside GPS, implementing encrypted and authenticated GPS signals, and employing advanced anomaly detection systems. Additionally, regular system audits, geofencing, manual override procedures, and collaboration with maritime regulatory bodies are crucial for enhancing navigational security and ensuring vessel safety against these cyber threats.

Regulations

There are several guidelines and regulations globally relevant to autonomous boats or submersibles:

- **International Maritime Organization (IMO):** The IMO aims to integrate new and advancing technologies in its regulatory framework. They conducted a regulatory scoping exercise on maritime autonomous surface ships (MASS) in 2021 to assess existing IMO instruments and how they might apply to ships that utilize varying degrees of automation. The aim is to adopt a non-mandatory goal-based MASS Code to take effect in 2025, which will form the basis for a mandatory goal-based MASS Code, expected to enter into force on 1 January 2028.

- **Interim Guidelines for MASS Trials:** The Maritime Safety Committee (MSC) approved Interim guidelines for MASS trials in June 2019. These guidelines stated that trials should be conducted in a manner that provides at least the same degree of safety, security, and protection of the environment as provided by the relevant instruments.

- **European Union (EU):** The EU has developed Operational Guidelines on trials of MASS. These guidelines have been developed for use in the interest of the protection of safety and security at sea and of the marine and coastal environment.

The emergence of autonomous naval vessels is transforming the maritime industry, offering enhanced efficiency and reduced operational risks. However, the adoption of these innovative technologies must be accompanied by a heightened awareness of the unique cybersecurity challenges they pose. To secure the future of autonomous boats and submersibles, stakeholders must collaborate to develop and implement robust cybersecurity measures.

Skyward Bound: The Cybersecurity Aspects of Drones and eVTOLs

"Regulations, customer acceptance, and cost will all determine whether the industry reaches its potential to disrupt global logistics or remains limited to isolated applications."
– McKinsey, from article *Drone Delivery: More Lift Than You Think*

Zipline is a Silicon Valley organization that was founded in 2014, with a mission to build a logistics system that serves all people equally. In 2016, Zipline began delivering blood and medical products via drones to remote areas in Rwanda. Zipline has subsequently expanded rapidly, operating in seven countries across three continents and has flown more than 50 million commercial autonomous miles. But what truly sets Zipline apart is its diverse delivery portfolio, including food, retail, agriculture products, and animal health products. Zipline ensures that essential supplies reach those who need them.

Zipline has developed two distinct platforms for delivery: one for long-range delivery and another for precise home delivery. This dual approach allows them to cater to a wide range of needs and locations. Their innovative approach has not gone unnoticed. Retail giant Walmart has partnered with Zipline for drone delivery launches. Customers can place orders through the Zipline app, and a Walmart associate hands the packaged product off to Zipline staff, who prepare the aircraft for launch.

But perhaps the most compelling aspect of Zipline's story is its impact. With its expansion to Ghana in 2019, Zipline became the world's largest medical drone-delivery service, reaching over 25 million people. Their services have been crucial in saving lives by ensuring timely delivery of essential medical supplies.

Zipline's story is a testament to the power of technology and innovation. It is a story of how a simple idea can transform lives and make a positive impact on society.

The aviation industry has witnessed a remarkable transformation with the advent of autonomous flying vehicles. Autonomous flying vehicles encompass a wide range of vehicles, from small consumer drones used for photography and recreation to large electric vertical take-off and landing vehicles (eVTOLs) designed for urban air mobility and cargo delivery. These vehicles rely on cutting-edge technology, including advanced sensors, AI-driven algorithms, and high-speed communication networks to operate safely and efficiently. These vehicles are also taking a more important role in modern warfare as seen during recent conflicts.

These innovations are revolutionizing transportation, logistics, and countless other industries. However, as with any technological advancement, there are specific cybersecurity challenges that need to be addressed to ensure the safety and security of these aerial vehicles.

- **Remote Hijacking and Unauthorized Access**: In 2021, researchers demonstrated the ability to hack into a military drone's GPS system, altering its flight path. This incident highlights the risk of remote hijacking and unauthorized access to drones and eVTOLs, which could lead to dangerous consequences. Autonomous flying vehicles rely on GPS and communication systems to navigate and receive commands. If these systems are compromised, it could allow hackers to take control of the vehicle, redirect it, or cause it to crash. Securing these communication channels and ensuring authentication and authorization protocols are robust is crucial.

- **Data Privacy and Surveillance**: Concerns have been raised about the use of drones for surveillance purposes, such as monitoring public gatherings or private properties. There have been cases of drones capturing sensitive personal information, posing privacy risks. Drones and eVTOLs are equipped with cameras and sensors, raising concerns about the invasion of privacy and unauthorized data collection. Strict regulations and ethical considerations are necessary to protect privacy rights and ensure responsible use of these technologies.

- **Jamming and Spoofing**: There are two main ways to interfere with drone and eVTOLs, the first being jamming, which is intentionally using a transmission-blocking signal to disrupt communications. Once a drone is jammed, it can be forced to land on the spot, halting any further movement, or return to its "home" location. The second is spoofing, which is when a third party takes over a drone remotely by impersonating the control signal. It involves emitting a signal that is supposed to confuse the drone so that it thinks the spoofing signal is legitimate (when in fact it is not).

In 2011, the Iranian government allegedly captured an American stealth drone by spoofing its GPS coordinates, tricking it into landing in Iran instead of its home base.

- **Physical Security:** In 2019, drones were used to drop explosives on an oil pipeline in Saudi Arabia. This attack highlights the potential for physical harm and damage that drones can cause when in the wrong hands. Ensuring physical security, including anti-tamper mechanisms and safeguards against drone-based attacks, is vital to protect critical infrastructure and public safety. Detection and interception systems should also be in place to counter malicious drone activities.

- **Firmware and Software Vulnerabilities:** In March 2023, researchers detected security vulnerabilities in several drones made by DJI, a Chinese technology organization. These vulnerabilities allowed users to change a drone's serial number or override the mechanisms that allow security authorities to track the drones and their users. In some cases, the drones could even be brought down remotely in flight.

  Firmware and software vulnerabilities pose a significant risk, as they can be exploited to compromise the integrity and functionality of autonomous flying vehicles. Regular updates and patches are essential to address these vulnerabilities and maintain the cybersecurity of these platforms.

- **Collision Avoidance Systems:** Autonomous drones have been known to fail to detect and avoid obstacles, resulting in collisions. This raises concerns about the reliability and security of these systems. Malfunctioning collision avoidance systems can lead to accidents, endangering lives. Ensuring the resilience of these systems, including redundancy measures, is crucial to prevent such incidents.

- **Supply Chain Security:** Autonomous flying vehicles rely on a complex supply chain that includes various components and software. Ensuring the security and integrity of the supply chain is crucial to prevent the introduction of malicious hardware or software into these systems.

- **Ethical Considerations:** The ethical use of autonomous flying vehicles is a growing concern. Decisions about how these vehicles are used, including their role in surveillance, law enforcement, and military applications, raise ethical questions that need careful consideration. The ethical considerations of the use of this technology will also shape the kinds of attacks and cybersecurity concerns any operator or manufacturer of these vehicles will encounter.

- **Regulatory and Compliance Challenges:** Establishing a robust regulatory framework for autonomous flying vehicles is essential to address cybersecurity concerns. Ensuring compliance with these regulations and industry standards is a challenge, but it is necessary to maintain safety and security. There is currently no universal set of unified rules that all countries agree on when it comes to drones.

The emergence of autonomous flying vehicles presents a promising future for transportation and logistics. However, addressing the cybersecurity challenges associated with these innovations is paramount to ensure their safe and secure operation. Feature stories have highlighted the vulnerabilities and risks, ranging from remote hijacking to privacy concerns and physical security threats.

Future Cybersecurity
Concerns with Autonomous Vehicles

"Our future success is directly proportional to our ability to understand, adopt, and integrate new technology into our work."
– Sukant Ratnakar, author of *Open the Windows*

The emergence of autonomous vehicles (AVs) presents significant opportunities and challenges. The journey of AVs, from the early experiments at Carnegie Mellon University to the pioneering advancements by organizations like NASA, Tesla, and Zipline, illustrates a trajectory of relentless innovation and boundless potential.

The autonomous future promises a world where transportation is more efficient and accessible while also being safer and more environmentally friendly. The implications of this technology extend beyond the convenience of driverless cars or the efficiency of unmanned delivery drones. They will impact urban environments, reshape industries, and redefine the concept of mobility and connectivity.

The most successful organizations in this space will be the ones that center their efforts on creating safe products. Producing safe, secure, and reliable autonomous vehicles will reassure reticent consumers, regulators, and investors and pave the way for market adoption of this new technology.

The autonomous future should be approached with cautious optimism, embracing the innovations AVs introduce while being acutely aware of the cybersecurity challenges they present.

While the challenges are significant, recent success stories in the field of autonomous vehicle cybersecurity offer hope and inspiration. These examples demonstrate that with the right approach and commitment, it is possible to secure the future of transportation:

- **Tesla's Bug Bounty Program:** This program is a shining example of how proactive companies can be in addressing cybersecurity concerns. They offer substantial rewards to security researchers who identify and report vulnerabilities, fostering a community of ethical hackers dedicated to improving the security of their vehicles.

- **Waymo's Safety and Security Approach:** Waymo places a strong emphasis on safety and security. Their multi-layered approach to cybersecurity includes continuous testing, vulnerability assessments, and a commitment to sharing safety data with the public.

- **Industry Partnerships:** Major automotive manufacturers are partnering with cybersecurity firms to enhance the security of autonomous vehicles. Recent collaborations between Ford and cybersecurity organization McAfee demonstrate a commitment to proactive cybersecurity measures.

Education and public perception will play pivotal roles. Just as society gradually adapted to the concept of automated elevators, so too must society evolve to embrace and trust autonomous vehicles. This transition will require time, transparency, and proof of safety and efficacy.

We are entering an exciting era in human history, where our roads, skies, and seas will be shared with intelligent machines. Cybersecurity will not just be a technical matter but a crucial aspect of public safety and trust.

Chapter 7

Immersive Worlds, Immersive Threats: VR, AR, and Metaverse Security

"We believe the metaverse will be the successor to the mobile internet;
we'll be able to feel present—like we're right there with people
no matter how far apart we actually are."
– Mark Zuckerberg, CEO Meta

Diving into the Virtual:
The Appeal and Threats of VR, AR,
and the Metaverse

"Virtual reality is the "ultimate empathy machine." These experiences are more than documentaries. They're opportunities to walk a mile in someone else's shoes."
– Chris Milk, entrepreneur

The origin of virtual reality (VR) can be traced back to the 1960s, with Morton Heilig's "Sensorama," an early VR machine, and Ivan Sutherland's "Ultimate Display." Yet, it was not until the exponential growth in computational power and graphics processing in the late 20th and early 21st centuries that VR and augmented reality (AR) began to fulfill their potential.

VR, once a concept of science fiction, is now a burgeoning reality, offering experiences beyond the physical world's limitations. AR and the metaverse further blur the lines between the physical and digital worlds. When the term virtual reality first appeared as a technology, it conjured up images of sci-fi wonder and futuristic play. Today, it holds promise as a potential technological evolution.

The appeal of these technologies is undeniable. VR is fully immersive, hijacking your senses and perception of time, transporting you to distant places or historical events with an intensity that defies physical limitations. For example, you can now "travel" to a bustling market in Cairo, Egypt, and explore the ruins of Chernobyl, Ukraine, both of which most people are unlikely to experience in person.

AR overlays digital information onto our real-world view, transforming how we interact with our immediate surroundings. In 2021, IKEA, the Swedish furniture store, built an AR app called IKEA Place using Apple's ARKit, a developer toolkit created to usher in the augmented reality revolution on iOS devices. The app allows you to browse an extensive catalogue of products, including sofas, armchairs, coffee tables, and storage units, then you can hold up your phone and, using the phone's camera, place the digital furniture anywhere in a room. While AR has already begun transforming our interactions with the physical world, as seen with apps like IKEA Place, another digital revolution is emerging that promises to further blur the lines between the physical and the digital—that being the metaverse.

The metaverse, a collective virtual shared space, promises a convergence of digital and in-person experiences. Think of a virtual space where your digital avatar can virtually live, work, and play. The Chief Disruptor at Deloitte aptly described the metaverse: "In the simplest terms, the metaverse is the internet, but in 3D." Before you assume that the metaverse is just hype, look no further than the already existing and successful games such as Fortnite by Epic Games, or Roblox. Many a parent has been perplexed by their children's request to receive their allowance in Robux, the virtual currency in Roblox, which allows for the purchase of virtual products like clothes for their avatars or advantages in games.

Security, Privacy, and Ethical Considerations: As these technologies become more pervasive, questions around cybersecurity, privacy, and ethics arise. Cybersecurity in virtual experiences takes concepts from traditional cybersecurity, like data encryption or network security, and it expands these into the virtual experiences and assets and your virtual persona.

In the early days of VR, cybersecurity concerns might have been limited to data breaches or system hacks—significant yet familiar issues. However, as the VR/AR interfaces have evolved to become more intuitive and human-centered, the nature of threats evolved alongside.

In 2016, a victim shared her experience of being virtually groped while playing the VR game "QuiVr" on SteamVR. Despite her gender-neutral avatar, she believes her feminine voice attracted the attention of another player, who proceeded to grope her avatar's chest and crotch. This incident led to public backlash against the perpetrator, who later changed his online identity and blamed the victim for the negative attention he received. This case underscores the issue of unbridled misogyny and the consequences of gaming anonymity.

As recently as January 2024, a minor in the UK was allegedly subjected to a virtual gang rape. The girl was reportedly wearing a virtual reality headset and playing an immersive game in the metaverse when her avatar was attacked by several others.

Research conducted by the Center for Countering Digital Hate (CCDH), in 2021, shows that VR Chat, the most reviewed social app in Meta's VR metaverse, is rife with abuse, harassment, racism, and pornographic content. The research found that users, including minors, are exposed to abusive behavior every seven minutes. Such incidents spoil user experiences but can also lead to real psychological distress and tangible financial loss.

The risk landscape has diversified to include deepfakes (fake manipulated videos that appear real), theft of biometric data, and the manipulation of sensory input to deceive or disorient users.

As these platforms collect more personal information, the stakes become significantly higher. VR headsets track not just what you do but how you move and react, biometric data that could be exploited to craft highly personalized and convincing phishing attacks. The AR applications, always aware of your physical environment, could become tools for surveillance if misused.

The story of cybersecurity in VR and AR is also a story of regulatory whack-a-mole, with policy consistently lagging behind technology. This was evident in the early commercial VR systems of the 2010s, which lacked comprehensive privacy policies, leaving user data vulnerable. The challenge persists today as the metaverse promises a level of data integration that exceeds anything we have previously managed. Some of the organizations leading the development and deployment of VR and metaverse experiences have some of the worst data privacy track records.

Moving on to the hardware, there has been a dramatic evolution of VR and AR hardware. From clunky headsets with a nest of wires, to sleek, standalone units, these devices have become more powerful and, at the same time, more vulnerable. Each camera, mic, or sensory improvement, and each stride toward more immersive experiences, opens new avenues for exploitation.

Confronting the cybersecurity risks inherent in VR, AR, and the metaverse, is challenged by the intersection of technology and psychology. Protecting digital data is as crucial as safeguarding the human psyche. The way forward demands vigilance, foresight, and a commitment to ethical principles.

Protecting Privacy and Data Security in Virtual Worlds

"I'm excited about augmented reality because, unlike virtual reality, which closes the world out, AR allows individuals to be present in the world but hopefully allows an improvement on what's happening presently."
– Tim Cook, CEO Apple Inc.

Virtual reality (VR) and augmented reality (AR) technologies have introduced a new era of immersive experiences, but they also pose unique privacy concerns. These devices can collect a wide array of sensitive user data. Meta's Oculus headset boasts that the headset features 6 degrees of freedom tracking, which means it can track the movement of both your head and body, then translate them into VR with realistic precision.

Apple's Vision Pro has an array of advanced cameras and sensors that work together to let you see the world clearly, understand your environment, and detect hand input. It reportedly features more than a dozen cameras and sensors to track your eyes, facial expressions, hands, and even legs. With these mind-blowing tracking capabilities, you are not just leaving behind traditional digital footprints, such as browsing history or purchase records, but also biometric data like eye tracking, facial expressions, and heart rate. Additionally, you are leaving environmental information behind, like full scans of your environment, including any books, letters, or anything left lying around your space. This is the ultimate surveillance technology. These pieces of information can reveal intimate details about your preferences, behaviors, and even emotional states.

The collection of such detailed personal data raises significant privacy concerns. The most obvious risk is that this data could be used to build even more accurate profiles of you, leading to targeted advertising that raises ongoing ethical questions about these practices. More concerning is the potential for this data to be used in ways that you may not have consented to, such as government surveillance or by insurance companies adjusting premiums based on perceived health risks, or worse, identity theft by cybercriminals.

Although many people may not have concerns about being specifically targeted, the crux of the matter lies in the security of the sensitive data that organizations collect. Breaches in data security often result in the exposure of personal information of all individual users, with potentially devastating consequences. The psychological impact of having personal and biometric data exposed can be profound, given the intimate nature of the information collected by VR and AR devices.

As VR and AR technologies continue to evolve, they also present new security vulnerabilities. These platforms are complex systems with multiple layers of software and hardware, each presenting potential entry points for cyber criminals. The integration of VR and AR with other smart devices, information systems, and IoT, further expands the attack surface, increasing the risk of misuse, unauthorized access, and data breaches.

In 2022, researchers at Rutgers University–New Brunswick discovered a vulnerability in VR headsets, where hackers could exploit the voice command feature. These "eavesdropping attacks" could allow hackers to record speech-associated facial dynamics via built-in motion sensors in the headsets. This could potentially lead to the theft of sensitive information communicated via voice command, including credit card data and passwords.

Protecting user data in VR and AR environments is challenging due to the real-time processing and transmission of data required for immersive experiences. Traditional security measures might not be sufficient or could degrade the user experience. For instance, heavy encryption might slow down data transmission, affecting the performance of VR/AR applications. This is where the use of edge computing will likely be very effective, even demanded by users.

There is a crucial role for policymakers in establishing clear guidelines and regulations for data security in VR and AR platforms. This includes defining standards for data handling, user consent, and data breach notifications. Cross-border data flow in these global platforms presents additional regulatory challenges that need to be addressed to ensure user data is protected worldwide. Regulations specifically targeting virtual environments and technologies seem unlikely. Therefore, it is important to depend on more general regulations such as data privacy and cybersecurity regulations.

VR and AR technologies certainly offer exciting possibilities; they also bring substantial privacy and data security challenges. Addressing these issues requires a concerted effort from technology developers and users to ensure that these innovative platforms are safe, secure, and respectful of user privacy.

Controlling Chaos: The Challenge of Content Regulation in the Metaverse

"Fake news and rumors thrive online because few verify what's real and always bias towards content that reinforces their own biases."
Ryan Higa, online comedian

One of the questions you may be asking is how organizations will manage inappropriate content. Moderating content on social media sites and the internet are challenging enough, and far from a solved problem. Content moderation in the metaverse will likely be more challenging.

The metaverse, as a conglomeration of virtual worlds and experiences, presents unique challenges in content moderation. Unlike traditional digital platforms, the metaverse involves real-time interactions in a three-dimensional space, making the monitoring and management of content more complex. The key challenge lies in balancing freedom of expression with the need to prevent harmful or illegal content.

Physical harassment is bad enough; now consider virtual harassment. Instances of harassment in virtual environments, such as a user's personal space being invaded in a VR social platform, highlight the need for effective moderation tools. Platforms like VRChat have implemented personal space features and reporting mechanisms to address this.

Another example is the proliferation of inappropriate content in user-generated environments. Platforms like Roblox, which allow user-generated content, have faced challenges in filtering out inappropriate creations, such as games with violent or adult themes. Roblox uses a combination of automated systems and human moderators to enforce its community standards.

As with social media platforms, there is the need for robust moderation systems that can rapidly identify and address inappropriate content. This involves a combination of AI-driven tools for real-time monitoring and human oversight to handle nuanced situations. Additionally, user empowerment is crucial, providing users with tools to control their experience and report violations.

VR and AR experiences, with their immersive and influential nature, can have a profound impact on young users. Ensuring that these experiences are age-appropriate is vital to protect children and adolescents from exposure to content that may be harmful to their development.

Examples of Age-Related Concerns

Exposure to Violent Content: Games like Beat Saber or Fortnite, when experienced in VR, provide more intense experiences than traditional gaming. This raises concerns about the impact of violent content on young users, requiring stricter age-rating systems for VR and AR content.

Psychological Impact of Immersive Experiences: Studies have shown that immersive experiences can have a stronger emotional and psychological impact. This is particularly important for children and adolescents, whose brains are still developing. Therefore, content creators and platforms need to be mindful of the potential impacts of their experiences on younger audiences.

Regulators and developers need to consider both the psychological and developmental aspects when creating age guidelines for VR and AR content. This might involve enhanced age verification systems, implementing more effective age verification methods to prevent minors from accessing inappropriate content. Age-specific content needs to be designed to be suitable for different age groups, considering the different cognitive and emotional development stages of users.

A collaborative approach involving policymakers, educators, psychologists, and technology developers is necessary to establish comprehensive guidelines for age-appropriate content in VR and AR. This includes not only setting age restrictions but also educating parents and guardians about the nature of these technologies and the importance of supervising their children's digital experiences.

Guidelines will obviously differ per country; take China as an example. China has imposed a series of restrictions on online gaming for minors to help prevent young people from becoming addicted to video games. Children under 18 are banned from playing online between 10 p.m. and 8 a.m. They are restricted to 90 minutes of gaming on weekdays and three hours on weekends and holidays. Children can game only on Fridays, Saturdays, Sundays, and national holidays, and only between 8 p.m. and 9 p.m. on those days. These rules may appear draconian, but perhaps China is directionally right. Time will tell.

There is no doubt that content regulation in the metaverse will pose many unique challenges; it also presents an opportunity to create a safer and more inclusive virtual world, making the technology more appealing to users, advertisers, and investors. Content regulation in the metaverse and in VR/AR platforms is a complex issue requiring a multifaceted approach. Balancing free expression with safety, especially for younger users, requires innovative solutions, international cooperation, and ongoing dialogue among various stakeholders.

Rethinking Ethics in Virtual Spaces

"When we talk about the metaverse, we're describing both a new platform and a new application type; similar to how we talked about the web and websites in the early 90s."
– Satya Nadella, CEO Microsoft

While organizations like Apple and Meta are developing their own hardware and carefully controlling the environments, Microsoft has joined the metaverse with perhaps one of the more compelling software products. In January 2024, Microsoft introduced a virtual platform called Mesh to the popular Microsoft Teams product. Think of this as the virtual future of Microsoft Teams meetings. This promises a break away from 2D online meetings, offering immersive 3D experiences from any desktop or VR headset. It is not clear how many people will want to spend more than an hour or two with a bulky headset on, but as the form factor gets smaller, lighter, and more capable, perhaps this virtual future will become more of a reality. To use Mesh, you don't need to wear a VR headset, but it is more immersive if you do. Microsoft has built a 2D version into Teams, with 2D users appearing as a webcam window inside a 3D environment, watching everyone else as 3D avatars.

As these virtual technologies become more sophisticated, they blur the lines between reality and virtuality. This convergence raises significant ethical considerations, particularly concerning the impact on mental health and social behavior.

The immersive nature of VR and AR can have profound psychological effects. For instance, prolonged exposure to virtual environments might lead to a disconnection from the real world, potentially exacerbating conditions like depression or social anxiety. On the flip side, VR therapy has been used effectively for treating phobias and PTSD, showcasing the dual-edged nature of these technologies.

Virtual environments also affect social behavior. They offer new forms of social interaction, which can be both beneficial and detrimental. For example, VR platforms like Second Life create spaces for socializing and exploring different aspects of identity, which can be empowering.

However, they can also lead to escapism or a preference for virtual interactions over real-life connections.

Ethicists and developers must consider these implications. They should aim to create balanced experiences that enrich users' lives without encouraging harmful levels of detachment from reality. Clear guidelines and recommendations for users on balancing virtual and real-world activities are essential.

In virtual environments, users mostly represent themselves through avatars. These digital personas can range from realistic representations to fantastical creations. The creation and use of avatars brings about ethical challenges related to identity and representation. There is the potential for misrepresentation, where users might feel pressured to conform to certain standards of beauty or behavior in their avatars. This can perpetuate unrealistic body images and stereotypes.

Avatars can also be a source of bias and discrimination. For instance, users might unconsciously replicate societal biases in their avatar choices, or they might face different treatment based on their avatar's appearance, mirroring real-world prejudices.

To address these issues, VR and AR platforms need to encourage diversity and inclusivity in avatar creation tools. This means offering a wide range of customization options that represent different body types, ethnicities, and abilities. Additionally, fostering a community culture that values diversity and respects all forms of digital identity is crucial.

Developers and policymakers play a critical role in shaping the norms around digital identity in virtual spaces. They need to be aware of the social and psychological impacts of digital representation and strive to create environments that promote healthy self-expression and interaction. In an organizational setting, it is not unrealistic to expect guidelines on avatar usage and requirements for staff to represent themselves as accurately as possible. For instance, Microsoft has implemented avatar policies for its Teams platform. Some of the key points that these policies include are:

- **Availability:** Admins can control whether avatars for Teams is available in their organizations.

- **Setup and Permissions:** Policies allow or block the avatars for Teams app in the organization.

- **User Groups:** By default, the global (Org-wide default) policy is applied to all users in the organization. More policies can be created for subsets of users, such as executives, sales, manufacturing, etc.

- **Installation:** Users need to manually install and pin the avatars for Teams app.

Microsoft employees have also shared their experiences and etiquette for using avatars in Teams meetings. They have found that personalization is key, and users want to represent themselves in accordance with their preferences.

As organizations increasingly use virtual environments for business activities, they are beginning to establish guidelines for employee avatar appearance. Some key points that these policies may include are:

- **Appearance:** Employees may be asked to moderate the appearance of their virtual characters, or "avatars," to conform to the organization's dress code policies. For instance, some organizations allow employees to have creative avatars if full names and titles are continually displayed.

- **Conduct:** Like webpages, blogs, and other social media, which are already frequently monitored and regulated by employers, the appearance and conduct of avatars can have effects on real-world employees and situations. It will likely be appropriate to extend existing codes of conduct, including policies against discrimination, harassment, and retaliation, to virtual environments.

- **Enforcement:** Employment discrimination laws require that employers establish uniform guidelines applicable to all employees. Any effort at regulating avatar appearance and behavior should apply equally to all employees.

- **Content-based Regulation:** Employers should take care not to develop avatar appearance requirements that could form the basis of a discrimination claim. For instance, restrictions that may give rise to a claim of religious discrimination, like bans on religious symbols, or age discrimination, like requiring avatars to reflect a more youthful image than real-life counterparts, should be avoided.

These policies are still evolving and vary widely among different organizations. They are expected to become more common as the use of virtual environments for business activities increases.

The ethical implications of VR and AR technologies are complex and multifaceted. As the boundaries between reality and virtuality blend, and as we confront the complexities of digital identity and representation, a collaborative and thoughtful approach is necessary. This approach should involve not only technology developers but also psychologists, sociologists, ethicists, and the users, to ensure that the technology is used in ways that are beneficial and respectful of human dignity and diversity.

The Future of Regulations in Virtual Spaces

"This metaverse is going to be far more pervasive and powerful than anything else. If one central company gains control of this, they will become more powerful than any government and be a God on Earth."
– Tim Sweeney, CEO of Epic Games

Virtual and augmented reality technologies are evolving fast and legal systems are generally unprepared. The regulatory landscape for virtual reality (VR), augmented reality (AR), and the metaverse is still in its infancy. Existing laws struggle to keep pace with technological advancements. Historically, laws and regulations over new technologies are determined by each country or economic block based on societal, judicial, and legislative forces. This model does not work as well for virtual environments as the whole concept is based on not needing to know where someone is physically located.

As virtual experiences become more prominent, it is important to acknowledge that the behaviors and conflicts that we encounter in real life will likely manifest in virtual environments too. This raises numerous questions that extend beyond current online challenges.

Navigating virtual behavior raises complex challenges from both legal and ethical perspectives. Traditional laws governing behaviors like indecency, fraud, and assault are now being tested in the virtual world, sparking debates about their applicability and enforcement in these new environments. A pivotal question arises: Should the responsibility for upholding contractual rights and regulating activities fall on the users, or should it be shouldered by the platform providers? The ambiguity extends to the rights users might relinquish within these platforms, especially when venturing into unique or unconventional virtual experiences.

The legal landscape becomes even more complex when considering the types of virtual behaviors that could warrant civil or criminal action. How should real-world law enforcement agencies tackle misconduct confined to the virtual world, and what measures can ensure equitable and just enforcement? Furthermore, the debate intensifies when evaluating virtual activities that lead to tangible real-world outcomes, like physical accidents or financial deceit, against those with more abstract impacts, such as emotional distress. The challenge of pinpointing legal jurisdiction for virtual conduct adds another layer of complexity, raising questions about the credibility and legal significance of virtual statements and actions.

Consider issues around joint liability, intellectual property rights, and the delicate balance between wealth accumulation, taxation, and insurance in the context of virtual interactions. Issues like defamation, unauthorized use or manipulation of personal likeness or voice, and the limits of technological enhancement come under scrutiny. Paramount to this discourse is the need to establish fundamental rules within virtual spaces to safeguard human rights and protect vulnerable groups. As vast quantities of highly personal data are generated within virtual environments, the imperative for enforcement of stringent data privacy regulations to control and secure such data is critical.

These considerations highlight the complexity of regulating virtual environments and the need for tailored, forward-thinking approaches to legal and ethical governance in the virtual world.

Several existing frameworks indirectly impact these technologies. The European Union's General Data Protection Regulation (GDPR) is a prime example of data protection legislation impacting VR/AR. It regulates the processing of personal data, requiring consent for data collection and granting users the right to access and delete their data. This has implications for VR/AR developers, particularly in how they handle user data. In the US, the California Consumer Privacy Act (CCPA), which is like the EU GDPR, gives California residents more control over the personal information collected by businesses, which includes data gathered through VR/AR platforms. The US, Digital Millennium Copyright Act (DMCA) impacts VR/AR content, especially regarding user-generated content and the use of copyrighted materials in virtual environments. The Americans with Disabilities Act (ADA) mandates reasonable accommodations for people with disabilities, a standard that could extend to the accessibility of VR/AR technologies.

In 2020, lawyers for a deaf man filed a lawsuit against one of the biggest electronics companies in the world. The lawsuit stated that the company had violated the Americans with Disabilities Act (ADA) because there was no captioning on the company's virtual reality (VR) content housed on its subscription service. The case was settled out of court with both parties having reached an agreement regarding captioning on the VR subscription platform. The company pledged to provide resources to support developers to caption their content.

The rapid evolution of VR, AR, and the metaverse demands dynamic and forward-thinking regulatory measures. Future regulations will likely need to address:

- **Data Security and Privacy:** Given the amount of personal data collected by VR/AR devices, future regulations may impose stricter data security requirements and data transparency. Data privacy laws could become more prevalent globally, and enforcement will extend to virtual environments.

- **Ethical Use of Technology:** Regulations may emerge focusing on the ethical use of VR/AR, such as guidelines for content moderation, preventing addiction, and ensuring virtual environments do not have adverse psychological effects.

- **Accessibility Standards:** With increasing recognition of the importance of digital accessibility, future laws may set specific standards for VR/AR technologies, ensuring they are accessible to all users, including those with disabilities.

- **Global Regulatory Cooperation**: Given the global nature of the metaverse, international cooperation will be crucial in developing consistent regulatory standards. This may involve the formation of international bodies or agreements specifically focused on digital spaces.

The current regulatory framework for VR, AR, and the metaverse is an evolving landscape, with existing laws providing a foundation. However, the unique challenges posed by these technologies require the development of new regulations and the adaptation of existing ones. Future regulations will likely focus on data protection, ethical use, accessibility, and international cooperation to ensure that these burgeoning technologies are safe, secure, and accessible for all users.

Chapter 8

Blockchain, Cryptocurrencies, NFTs, and Smart Contracts

"We have proposed a system for electronic transactions without relying on trust. We started with the usual framework of coins made from digital signatures, which provides strong control of ownership but is incomplete without a way to prevent double-spending. To solve this, we proposed a peer-to-peer network using Proof of Work to record a public history of transactions that quickly becomes computationally impractical for an attacker to change if honest nodes control a majority of CPU power."

– Satoshi Nakamoto, referred to as the "father of Bitcoin," is the pseudonymous person or group of people who developed Bitcoin and authored the Bitcoin white paper.

Understanding Virtual Assets

*The main advantage of blockchain technology is supposed to be
that it's more secure, but new technologies are generally hard for people to trust,
and this paradox can't really be avoided."*
— Vitalik Buterin, co-founder of Ethereum

The advent of blockchain, non-fungible tokens (NFTs), and cryptocurrencies has introduced a revolution in technology. Although some have dismissed these technologies as scams, and indeed there have been numerous scams along the way, these groundbreaking innovations have revolutionized industries, unlocked new possibilities, and empowered individuals in unexpected ways.

Blockchain: The Foundation of Virtual Assets

The story of blockchain's invention is interesting. The idea behind blockchain technology can be traced back to 1991 when Stuart Haber and W. Scott Stornetta described the first work on a cryptographically secured chain of blocks. In 1992, they incorporated Merkle trees or hash trees into the design, allowing several documents to be collected into a block.

However, the concept of a blockchain-like protocol was first proposed even earlier, in 1982, by cryptographer David Chaum in his dissertation, "Computer Systems Established, Maintained, and Trusted by Mutually Suspicious Groups."

The primary breakthrough came with the invention of Bitcoin, the first cryptocurrency, which was launched in January 2009 by a person or group of people under the pseudonym Satoshi Nakamoto. Nakamoto's 2008 white paper revealed the blockchain system that would become the backbone of the cryptocurrency market. This marked the beginning of the blockchain revolution we see today. Blockchain technology has since been adopted in various sectors, from finance to health care, demonstrating its transformational potential.

Blockchains are decentralized and distributed ledger technologies that record transactions across multiple computers in a secure and tamper-resistant manner. This is achieved by utilizing cryptographic techniques, making it impossible for anyone to alter the data stored on the blockchain without consensus from the network. A blockchain is the opposite of traditional systems where data is stored on a central server, owned by a single organization, making it vulnerable to hacking and manipulation.

Blockchain technology is the backbone of cryptocurrencies like Bitcoin and Ethereum. It enables these digital currencies to function without the need for traditional intermediaries like banks. The blockchain's transparency, security, and immutability have gained the trust of users worldwide, driving the adoption for various purposes, including investments, online transactions, and as a store of value.

Cryptocurrencies: Digital Money for a Decentralized World

Cryptocurrencies are digital or virtual currencies that leverage blockchain technology to facilitate secure and transparent transactions. Unlike traditional fiat currencies issued by governments, cryptocurrencies are not controlled by any central authority. Since the launch of Bitcoin, thousands of cryptocurrencies have emerged, each with unique features and use cases. Some of the other established cryptocurrencies include Ethereum, Ripple, Litecoin, Solana, and Tether.

The decentralized nature of cryptocurrencies brings about several benefits, such as lower transaction fees, faster cross-border payments, and increased financial inclusivity. However, this decentralization also introduces a set of challenges for cybersecurity, as individuals are responsible for securing their digital assets, and there is no central authority to turn to in the event of a security breach or fraud.

NFTs: Digital Ownership in the Digital Age

Non-fungible tokens (NFTs) are a specific application of blockchain technology that has garnered attention in recent years. NFTs represent ownership of unique digital assets, such as digital art, music, videos, virtual real estate, and in-game items. Unlike cryptocurrencies, which are fungible and can be exchanged on a one-to-one basis, NFTs are indivisible and cannot be exchanged on a like-for-like basis.

The allure of NFTs lies in their ability to prove the authenticity, rarity, and ownership of digital assets in a digital world filled with replicas and copies. This has opened new opportunities for artists, content creators, and collectors to monetize their digital creations and engage with a global audience.

Smart Contracts: Automating Trust and Efficiency

Smart contracts are self-executing contracts with the terms of the agreement directly written into code. They are a pivotal feature of blockchain technology, particularly in platforms like Ethereum. These contracts automatically enforce and execute the terms of a contract when predefined conditions are met, without the need for intermediaries.

Smart contracts are the building blocks for decentralized applications (dApps) and have a wide range of applications, from automating complex business processes to creating decentralized autonomous organizations (DAOs). They facilitate trustless transactions, meaning parties can engage in agreements without needing to trust each other or a third party.

Smart contracts have the potential to revolutionize various industries by streamlining processes, reducing costs, and enhancing transparency. In finance, they enable complex financial instruments like decentralized finance (DeFi) applications. In supply chain management, they can be used to automate payments and verify the authenticity of products. Similarly, in real estate, smart contracts can simplify property transactions, reducing the need for intermediaries and paperwork.

Smart contracts represent a significant step forward in automating and securing digital transactions. As blockchain technology matures, the use and sophistication of smart contracts are expected to grow, offering more robust and efficient ways to facilitate digital agreements.

Blockchain Security Measures: Safeguarding the Immutable Ledger

"Blockchain is moving beyond cryptocurrency, and it's worth paying attention,
especially since successful prototypes show that blockchain,
also known as distributed ledger technology, will be transformative."
— Julie Sweet, Accenture CEO

Blockchain security is all about safeguarding the integrity and functionality of blockchain networks. It involves a combination of cybersecurity frameworks, assurance services, and best practices to mitigate the risk of attacks and fraud. The security of a blockchain network hinges on three fundamental principles that are worth mentioning: cryptography, decentralization, and consensus mechanisms.

- **Cryptography:** At its core, blockchain security relies heavily on cryptographic techniques. Each block in the chain is secured with cryptographic hashes, essentially digital fingerprints, that are unique and tamper evident. This cryptographic chaining ensures that any alteration of transaction data within a block is easily detectable, as it would require recalculating all subsequent block hashes, which is a near-impossible feat given the computational power required.

- **Decentralization:** Decentralization distributes the storage of data across a network of nodes. This dispersal eliminates single points of failure, a vulnerability common in centralized systems. In a blockchain network, compromising a single node, or even several nodes, doesn't jeopardize the entire network, making it inherently more resilient against attacks.

- **Consensus Mechanisms:** Consensus mechanisms are the processes by which transactions are validated and agreed upon by the network. Mechanisms like proof of work (PoW) and proof of stake (PoS) ensure that all participants agree on the transaction record. This collective validation acts as a deterrent against fraudulent activities, as altering transaction data would require overpowering the consensus of the entire network. While PoW and PoS are the most common consensus mechanisms, there are also others like delegated proof of stake (DPoS), proof of authority (PoA), and byzantine fault tolerance (BFT) variants, each with their own strengths and weaknesses.

The 51% Attack

Although blockchains, with their distributed nature, may seem impervious to compromise, this assumption is not entirely accurate. In a 51% attack, if an entity would gain control of over 50% of a blockchain network's computing power, they would be able to manipulate the ledger.

One of the most well-known 51% attacks occurred in 2020 when Ethereum Classic (ETC) was targeted multiple times. The attackers managed to control more than 51% of the network's mining power, enabling them to perform double-spending attacks, resulting in millions of dollars in losses for exchanges and other stakeholders.

The ETC attacks underscored the need for improved blockchain security measures:

- **Enhanced Hashrate Distribution:** The concentration of mining power in a few large pools made ETC vulnerable. Encouraging an even distribution of hashrate among miners can mitigate such attacks.

- **Consensus Algorithm Improvements:** Exploring alternative consensus mechanisms or hybrid systems that are less susceptible to 51% attacks.

- **Community Vigilance:** A vigilant blockchain community can detect and respond to potential threats more effectively. Communication and coordination among developers, miners, and users are crucial.

The Foundation of Blockchain Security

- **Immutable Ledger:** One of the key attractions of blockchain is its immutability. Once data is recorded on the blockchain, it is extremely challenging to alter or delete. Implementing robust mechanisms to maintain this immutability is crucial. Blockchain developers use cryptographic hashes and timestamping to create a secure and unchangeable record of transactions.

- **Securing the Network:** Blockchain nodes are the backbone of the network. For major node operators, ensuring the security of these nodes is paramount. Node operators must regularly update their software to patch vulnerabilities. Additionally, firewalls, intrusion detection systems, and access controls should be implemented to protect against unauthorized access.

The choice of consensus mechanism impacts security. While PoW is secure but energy-intensive, PoS is energy-efficient but requires a significant stake, which is a certain amount of cryptocurrency held as collateral. Properly configuring these mechanisms and addressing potential attack vectors is essential.

- **Public and Private Keys:** Users interact with the blockchain using cryptographic keys. Managing these keys securely is fundamental. Implementing multi-signature wallets, hardware wallets, and secure key storage practices are essential to prevent unauthorized access. This will be covered in more detail later.

- **Access Control:** For private or industry specific blockchains, access control mechanisms ensure that only authorized users can participate in blockchain transactions.

- **Upgrades:** Upgrades and modifications to blockchains are implemented through processes known as forks—either hard forks or soft forks. Hard forks represent significant changes to the blockchain's protocol, making the new rules incompatible with the old. They require all users to upgrade to the latest version of the software to continue participating. Hard forks are crucial for the evolution and improvement of blockchain networks, they can be sources of contention within the community. This was notably observed in the Bitcoin and Ethereum communities, where hard forks led to disagreements and even resulted in separate, competing blockchains. The key to successfully navigating hard forks lies in meticulous planning and effective communication among network participants to avoid splits and maintain network stability.

On the other hand, soft forks are a more subtle form of upgrade that maintains backward compatibility. This means that nodes running older versions of the software can still operate and validate new transactions, even if they do not support the new rules. However, for a soft fork to be successful, most of the network's miners need to adopt the upgrade. Soft forks also require careful coordination and consensus within the community. An illustrative example of a soft fork is Ethereum's transition from a PoW consensus mechanism to a PoS system. This change, while aiming to enhance efficiency and scalability, sparked extensive debates and highlighted the complexities involved in managing changes in a decentralized network.

Blockchain security is an ongoing challenge, with emerging threats and vulnerabilities constantly evolving. To safeguard the immutable ledger that blockchain promises, it is imperative to implement a multifaceted security strategy.

Cryptocurrency Cybersecurity Challenges

"Bitcoin is a remarkable cryptographic achievement, and the ability to create something that is not duplicable in the digital world has enormous value."
– Eric Schmidt, ex-Google CEO

Although blockchain and cryptocurrencies present numerous benefits, it is crucial to acknowledge the inherent cybersecurity risks that accompany them. There are numerous instances of hacking, fraud, and theft in the cryptocurrency market, highlighting the need for robust security measures. These risks are compounded by the fact that blockchain technology is relatively new, and there is a lack of regulatory frameworks governing its use.

Exchange Security

A cryptocurrency exchange is an online platform that facilitates the buying, selling, and trading of digital currencies such as Bitcoin and Ethereum. It operates similarly to a stock exchange, providing various trading and investing tools to its users. At the time of writing, some of the most popular cryptocurrency exchanges were Binance, Coinbase, and Kraken.

Not surprisingly, these exchanges have become lucrative targets for cybercriminals. Numerous exchanges have fallen victim to significant security breaches, resulting in the loss of billions of dollars' worth of cryptocurrencies and, in some instances, failure of the exchange itself. Take, for example, the case of the Italian cryptocurrency exchange Altsbit. In early 2020, Altsbit suffered a devastating cyberattack, leading to the closure of the exchange after a substantial portion of user funds were stolen. This incident was a wake-up call, emphasizing the vulnerability of even the more established exchanges to security breaches.

The challenges faced by cryptocurrency exchanges extend beyond external threats and cyberattacks. The collapse of FTX, one of the world's largest cryptocurrency exchanges in 2022, is a severe example. The FTX saga, involving allegations of mismanagement and misuse of customer funds, not only led to significant financial losses but also shook the confidence of investors and users in the stability and integrity of cryptocurrency exchanges.

In December 2022, the U.S. Securities and Exchange Commission (SEC) charged the FTX CEO, Bankman-Fried, with orchestrating a scheme to defraud equity investors in FTX. He was accused of diverting FTX customers' funds to his privately held crypto hedge fund, Alameda Research. The charges included fraud, conspiracy to commit money laundering, and conspiracy to defraud the US and violate campaign finance laws.

The Altsbit and FTX incidents highlight the risks inherent in centralized cryptocurrency exchanges. These examples underscore the importance of robust cybersecurity and regulations for cryptocurrency exchanges.

Wallet Security

If you possess any cryptocurrency, you have two options for storage. One is to keep the currency on an exchange, like a bank account. The other option is to store the currency in a wallet, a method known as self-custody. A cryptocurrency wallet is a digital tool that allows users to securely store, send, and receive digital currencies, such as Bitcoin or Ethereum. Unlike a physical wallet, a cryptocurrency wallet does not exactly store money, but rather it saves the cryptographic information (private keys) needed to access and manage digital assets on their respective blockchains.

A private key is a sophisticated form of cryptography that enables a user to access their cryptocurrency. It is like a password but far more secure. This key is what keeps your digital assets secure and, if compromised, can lead to unauthorized access to your funds. The ownership of cryptocurrency, therefore, is intrinsically tied to whoever possesses this private key. Ensuring the security of your private key is paramount in protecting your digital wealth. If someone gains access to, guesses, calculates, derives, or in any way utilizes your private key, they gain control over your cryptocurrencies, making them their own. Given the crucial nature of the private key, it is essential to ensure its security. To highlight this point, advocates of cryptocurrency like to remind users, "Not your keys, not your coins."

Cryptocurrency wallets are digital or physical tools that store and manage your private keys. They can be online (hot) or offline (cold). Online wallets are connected to the internet and offer more accessibility but also present higher risks of being hacked. Cold wallets, on the other hand, are not connected to the internet, making them less vulnerable.

It is worth exploring the different types of cryptocurrency wallets, each with unique features and levels of security:

- **Software Wallets:** These are programs that can be installed on a computer (desktop wallet) or mobile phone (mobile wallet). Some of the leading brands in this category are Exodus, Electrum, and Mycelium. They offer convenient access to digital assets but may be vulnerable to malware attacks.

- **Hardware Wallets:** These are physical devices designed to secure cryptocurrency. They are offline and thus provide increased security. Some of the leading brands are Trezor, Ledger, and KeepKey. It is important to buy hardware wallets from reputable sources to avoid counterfeit devices. While ensuring protection against online attacks, it is important to maintain the safety of your hardware device and remember your passphrase.

- **Web or Online Wallets:** These wallets run on the cloud and are accessible from any computing device in any location. Some of the leading brands are Blockchain.com, Coinbase, and Binance. They offer convenient access but may be vulnerable to hacking attacks.

- **Paper Wallets:** The term paper wallet usually refers to a physical printout of a user's private keys. These are easy to use and provide a very high level of security, assuming the paper is never lost, stolen, or destroyed.

- **Custodial Wallets:** These are services where the private key to a wallet is kept by a third party. Leading brands include Coinbase, BitGo, and Gemini. They offer convenience but are not considered very secure since users do not have full control of their private keys.

It is essential to understand the different types of wallets and choose carefully based on the level of security and convenience that you require. Although it may initially appear overwhelming, the concept is not vastly different from traditional banking or physical wallets, where diverse options exist for storing and accessing funds. Ultimately, it is your responsibility to ensure the safety of your digital assets by choosing a trusted wallet and following best practices such as setting strong passwords and enabling two-factor authentication.

As wallet security has improved, cybercriminals have resorted to exploiting user vulnerability, giving rise to the prevalence of phishing and social engineering. Cybercriminals frequently employ sophisticated tactics to deceive users into divulging their private keys or login credentials, ultimately resulting in unauthorized access to wallets and the theft of digital assets.

The complexities of cryptocurrency trading and storage require a proactive approach towards security. The incidents involving FTX and other exchanges serve as a reminder of the importance of securing your digital assets. Central to this security is the understanding and safeguarding of your private keys. The variety of wallets available today offer a range of security and convenience features; however, your vigilance should not stop at choosing the right wallet. As the threat landscape evolves, so too must your awareness and action to protect yourself from cybercriminal tactics such as phishing and social engineering. In essence, the onus of safeguarding digital wealth lies primarily with you, the user. Use and adopt cryptocurrencies with caution, understanding, and a commitment to personal security.

Cryptojacking: The Unwanted Miner

"In a sense, cryptojacking is a way for cybercriminals to make free money with minimal effort. Cybercriminals can simply hijack someone else's machine with just a few lines of code. This leaves the victim bearing the cost of the computations and electricity that are necessary to mine cryptocurrency."
— Vitalik Buterin, co-founder of Ethereum

Cryptocurrency mining is a process akin to solving complex puzzles. Miners use powerful computers to solve intricate mathematical problems that validate and record transactions on the blockchain. Each time a miner successfully solves one of these problems, they are rewarded with a small amount of cryptocurrency. This reward serves as an incentive for miners to contribute their computing power to the network. The process is energy-intensive and requires significant computing resources, making it a sophisticated yet essential component of maintaining the integrity and functionality of networks.

Cybercriminals have taken advantage of this by devising a way to mine cryptocurrencies without owning or investing in expensive equipment. Cryptojacking, also referred to as malicious cryptomining, involves the illicit utilization of another individual's computational assets for cryptocurrency mining purposes. This insidious, difficult-to-detect form of cyberattack involves the unauthorized deployment of malicious code to hijack a victim's device to harness its computational power for the purpose of mining cryptocurrencies. While cryptojacking itself is not inherently malicious, the unauthorized use of a victim's resources for mining poses a threat to individuals and organizations alike.

In 2022, there was an average of 15.02 million cryptojacking cases per month, marking an 86% increase from the previous year's average of 8.09 million per month. On average, cryptojacking domains are short-term with over 20% having a lifespan of less than nine days.

The Mechanics of Cryptojacking

Cryptojacking typically begins when a victim inadvertently interacts with malicious content. This could be through clicking on a compromised link, visiting an infected website, or downloading a seemingly innocent file.

Once the malicious code gains access to the victim's device, it sets in motion a sequence of events.

First, the malware begins to run in the background, utilizing the device's processing unit to perform complex cryptographic calculations, which are an integral part of cryptocurrency mining. These calculations are resource-intensive and require a significant amount of computational power. As a result, the victim's device experiences a slowdown, increased power consumption, and a potential decrease in its overall lifespan due to the constant strain on its components. When businesses' cloud environments are targeted, cryptojacking can lead to substantial financial losses due to the spike in resource usage, directly impacting operational costs.

Second, the mined cryptocurrency is siphoned off to the attacker's wallet, serving as a clandestine source of income. The victim remains unaware of this illicit activity until they notice the adverse effects on their device's performance or take measures to investigate the issue.

To illustrate the gravity of the cryptojacking threat, consider the Coinhive incident. Coinhive was a popular cryptocurrency mining service that allowed website owners to monetize their content by using visitors' CPU power to mine the cryptocurrency, Monero. While it had legitimate uses, Coinhive became infamous for its misuse by cybercriminals.

Coinhive's service was designed to be embedded into websites with the consent of visitors, who would knowingly contribute their CPU resources to support the website. However, many malicious actors exploited this technology for their nefarious purposes. They injected Coinhive's mining script into compromised websites, turning the unsuspecting visitors into involuntary cryptocurrency miners.

One prominent case involved the popular torrent website, The Pirate Bay. In 2017, it was discovered that The Pirate Bay had embedded Coinhive's mining script without informing users. Millions of visitors unknowingly contributed their computational power to mine Monero for the website's operators. This incident sparked outrage and led to discussions about the ethics and legality of cryptojacking.

The Coinhive incident is just one example of the pervasive threat of cryptojacking. Over the years, cryptojackers have found creative ways to deploy their malicious code, targeting a wide range of victims. Some attackers have focused on compromising websites, while others have distributed malicious apps or used phishing campaigns to trick users into downloading cryptojacking malware.

In 2018, cybersecurity firm Palo Alto Networks uncovered a cryptojacking campaign known as "Graboid." This campaign infected over 2,000 Docker hosts, which is a popular containerization technology used in cloud computing. By exploiting a misconfiguration in the Docker API, the attackers were able to deploy malicious containers that mined Monero. The Graboid incident highlighted the vulnerability of cloud infrastructure to cryptojacking attacks, and it underscores the need for robust security measures in cloud-based environments.

Mitigating the Cryptojacking Threat

As cryptojacking continues to evolve, individuals and organizations must take proactive steps to protect themselves. There are several essential strategies to effectively counter the threat of cryptojacking:

- **Implement Robust Security Measures:** Employ reliable antivirus software, intrusion detection systems, and firewall solutions to detect and block cryptojacking attempts.

- **Use of Advanced Threat Detection Tools:** Utilize advanced threat detection tools that use machine learning and behavioral analysis to detect anomalies that traditional antivirus software might miss.

- **Regularly Update Software:** Keep all operating systems, browsers, and software up to date to patch known vulnerabilities that cryptojackers may exploit.

- **Monitor System Performance:** Regularly monitor device performance for any unusual spikes in CPU usage, which may indicate cryptojacking activity.

- **Cloud Resource Utilization Monitoring:** For organizations utilizing cloud services, it is important to monitor cloud resource utilization. An unexpected increase in resource usage can indicate that cryptojacking malware is running in the cloud environment.

- **Adopt Browser Extensions:** Install browser extensions that block cryptocurrency mining scripts, providing an added layer of defense when browsing the web.

- **Restrict Script Execution:** In addition to browser extensions, consider implementing web filtering solutions that can restrict the execution of unauthorized scripts on websites. This can be particularly useful in preventing drive-by cryptojacking where mining scripts are embedded in web pages.

- **Implement Application Whitelisting:** Application whitelisting can prevent unauthorized applications, including cryptojacking malware, from executing in the first place.

Cryptojacking, the unwanted miner, poses an important and evolving cybersecurity threat, as illustrated by the Coinhive and Graboid cases. Cryptojackers are persistent and creative in their methods. Awareness and proactive measures are crucial for individuals and organizations to defend against cryptojacking. By staying vigilant and implementing robust security measures, you can protect your devices and systems from becoming unwitting tools in the hands of cryptojackers.

NFTs and Cybersecurity: Owning Digital Art Safely

"Art is anything you can get away with."
– Marshall McLuhan, Canadian philosopher

In 2021, the digital art world was taken by surprise when a relatively unknown graphic designer named Mike Winkelmann, better known as Beeple, catapulted to fame in a way that would forever change the perception of digital art and non-fungible tokens (NFTs).

Beeple was no stranger to digital art, having committed to creating and posting a new piece of artwork online every day since 2007. This daily ritual, known as "Everydays," was Beeple's way of improving his skills and discipline. For years, he built up a vast collection of varied, quirky, and often provocative digital art pieces. In 2021, his dedication took an unexpected and lucrative turn.

In March 2021, Christie's, the renowned auction house, took an interest in Beeple's work, specifically a collage titled "Everydays: The First 5000 Days." This piece was a mosaic of the first 5000 days of his "Everydays" project. But what made this artwork unique was that it was created as an NFT.

NFTs, which certify the ownership and uniqueness of digital items using blockchain technology, were gaining traction, but Beeple's piece was about to skyrocket their popularity. The auction at Christie's was a landmark event, not only because it was one of the first instances of a major auction house selling a purely digital piece of art, but also due to the staggering final bid. "Everydays: The First 5000 Days" sold for an astonishing $69 million.

This sale was more than just a financial triumph; it signaled a paradigm shift in how digital art was perceived and valued. The world began to see the potential of NFTs to authenticate, own, and trade digital art, much like traditional art. Beeple's success ushered in a new era where digital creations could be as valuable, if not more, than physical art.

However, the story of Beeple and his NFT feat also opened a Pandora's box of sorts. The environmental concerns regarding the energy consumption of blockchain technology, along with the volatility of the crypto market and the potential for NFTs in scams and copyright issues, became hot topics.

Beeple himself remained somewhat grounded amidst this whirlwind. He saw his sudden rise not just as a personal achievement but as a validation of digital art as a legitimate and valuable form of creative expression.

Non-fungible tokens (NFTs) have emerged as a novel and exciting development and extension of blockchain technologies. NFTs enable the ownership and transfer of unique digital assets, like art, music, and virtual real estate. The allure of NFTs lies in their ability to provide provenance and scarcity to digital creations. Artists and content creators can now monetize their digital works by tokenizing them as NFTs, enabling them to sell and trade their art on blockchain-based NFT marketplaces (OpenSea, Rarible, Binance). Collectors, in turn, can prove ownership of these unique items by holding the corresponding NFT or token.

While NFTs represent ownership of digital assets, they are not stored directly on your device or personal computer. Instead, they reside on the blockchain and are accessed through digital wallets, the same wallets covered earlier. These wallets store the private keys needed to manage and trade your NFTs. Therefore, securing your digital wallet is paramount in the NFT ecosystem. The loss or theft of private keys can result in the irreversible loss of access to your NFTs. It is crucial to use trusted wallet providers and implement robust security measures like strong passwords and two-factor authentication to safeguard your digital assets.

Finally, an often overlooked yet critical aspect of NFT security is the regular backup of your digital wallet's private keys. These keys are your access point to your NFTs, and losing them means losing access to your assets. Regular backups, stored securely and preferably offline, provide a safety net against potential digital wallet failures or cyberattacks. Ensuring that you have a recoverable copy of your keys can save you from the distress of permanently losing your valuable digital art.

Scams in the NFT Space

Due diligence is essential when purchasing NFTs to avoid falling prey to scams. The burgeoning market has seen its share of fraudulent activities, including counterfeit NFTs and fake sales. Scammers may create NFTs that mimic popular artists or invent fictitious creator profiles. Before purchasing, verify the authenticity of the NFT, research its transaction history, and confirm the legitimacy of the creator. This vigilance protects your investment and ensures that you support genuine artists and creators in the digital space.

Another crucial aspect to consider is the legal dimension, particularly regarding copyright issues. Owning an NFT does not automatically grant copyright of the underlying digital art. It typically confers only ownership of a specific token representing the art. Misunderstanding this can lead to copyright infringements, as buyers might unlawfully reproduce or distribute the digital content. Navigating these legal complexities requires a clear understanding of what your NFT ownership entails and respecting the original creator's intellectual property rights.

Owning Digital Art Safely in the NFT World

As NFTs continue to gain traction, it is crucial for users to take proactive measures to protect themselves from NFT cybersecurity threats. On the next page are some best practices for owning digital art safely.

- **Use Reputable NFT Marketplaces:** When buying or selling NFTs, choose established and reputable NFT marketplaces with a track record of security and user protection. Research the marketplace's security measures and community reviews before engaging in transactions.

- **Beware of Suspicious Links and Downloads:** Be cautious when clicking on links or downloading files related to NFTs, especially if they come from unverified sources. Verify the legitimacy of the source before taking any action.

- **Employ Security Software:** Utilize reputable antivirus and anti-malware software to protect your device from cryptojacking and other malicious threats. Keep your security software up to date to detect and prevent emerging threats.

- **Regularly Update Software and Plugins:** Ensure that your operating system, web browser, and browser plugins are up to date with the latest security patches.

- **Educate Yourself:** Stay informed about the latest cybersecurity threats in the NFT space. Educate yourself on common attack vectors and phishing tactics to recognize potential threats.

- **Enable Two-Factor Authentication (2FA):** Whenever possible, enable 2FA on your NFT marketplace accounts and associated wallets. This provides an additional layer of security to protect your assets.

The rise of NFTs has introduced exciting opportunities for artists, collectors, and enthusiasts in the digital art world. However, it has also attracted cybercriminals looking to exploit the newfound enthusiasm for their illicit gain.

Smart Contract Vulnerabilities: The Devil's in the Details

"Trust but verify."
— Ronald Reagan, 40th president of the United States

Imagine you are in the bustling city of New York, looking to buy a beautiful apartment overlooking Central Park. You have found the perfect place, but the process of buying property is daunting, filled with paperwork, brokers, and endless waiting. Enter the world of smart contracts.

Propy, a real estate organization, has adopted smart contracts to enhance their services. With Propy, the entire process of buying your dream apartment becomes seamless. The smart contract, stored on the blockchain, contains all the terms of the agreement. Once you transfer the funds, the contract automatically executes, transferring the property title to you. There is no need for brokers or lawyers; the process is transparent, secure, and efficient.

Now, let us say you are not ready to buy, but you are looking for a place to rent. SMARTRealty is another organization that uses smart contracts for rental agreements. The terms of the lease are coded into a smart contract. If you pay your rent on time, the contract allows you to stay. If not, the contract could automatically enforce the eviction process. It is a straightforward system that reduces disputes and ensures both parties stick to their agreement.

Understanding Smart Contracts

Smart contracts are self-executing agreements with the terms of the contract directly written into code. They are deployed on blockchain platforms like Ethereum, where they automatically execute when predefined conditions are met. These contracts eliminate the need for intermediaries, making transactions faster, cheaper, and more transparent.

Smart contracts can be used for a wide range of applications, including token sales, supply chain management, and automated financial agreements. However, the same characteristics that make them attractive also make them susceptible to certain vulnerabilities.

- **Code Vulnerabilities:** Smart contracts are only as secure as the code they are written in. Any flaws or vulnerabilities in the code can be exploited by attackers. Common coding mistakes such as buffer overflows, integer overflows, and reentrancy bugs can lead to severe security breaches. Even a single line of incorrect code can have catastrophic consequences.

To illustrate the significance of code vulnerabilities, consider the case of the "Parity Wallet" incident. In July 2017, a vulnerability in a multi-signature wallet smart contract, deployed by Parity Technologies, allowed an attacker to lock up over 513,000 Ether (ETH), valued at approximately $300 million at the time. The vulnerability was a simple oversight in the code, highlighting how even experienced developers can make consequential mistakes.

- **The DAO Hack:** The DAO, short for "Decentralized Autonomous Organization," was a groundbreaking project launched in April 2016 on the Ethereum blockchain. It was designed to be a venture capital fund, allowing participants to vote on investment proposals using smart contracts. The DAO raised over $150 million worth of Ether, making it one of the most significant crowdfunding projects in history.

In June 2016, an attacker exploited a vulnerability in the DAO's smart contract code. The flaw allowed the attacker to repeatedly withdraw Ether from the DAO, draining it of around one-third of its funds, equivalent to around $50 million. This incident sent shockwaves through the Ethereum community and led to a contentious hard fork of the Ethereum blockchain to reverse the effects of the hack.

The DAO hack serves as a reminder of the potential vulnerabilities within even the most ambitious and well-funded blockchain projects. It served as a reminder to the entire industry, sparking conversations about code audits, security practices, and the need to exercise caution when deploying smart contracts.

- **Solidity Language Pitfalls:** Solidity is the most used programming language for writing Ethereum smart contracts. While it is a powerful tool, it comes with its own set of pitfalls. Developers who are not well-versed in Solidity may inadvertently introduce vulnerabilities into their smart contracts. Inadequate understanding of the language's nuances can lead to security issues like reentrancy attacks, as seen in the DAO hack.

- **Reentrancy Attacks:** A reentrancy attack occurs when a malicious contract calls back into the vulnerable contract, potentially manipulating its state or extracting funds. The most notorious example of a reentrancy attack is the DAO hack.

The aftermath of the DAO hack brought several important lessons to light:

- **Code Standards:** The development community has established coding standards and best practices for writing secure smart contracts in languages like Solidity. Following these standards can reduce the likelihood of vulnerabilities.

- **Security Audits:** Smart contract developers must prioritize security audits and code reviews by experienced professionals. Third-party audits can help identify vulnerabilities and mitigate risks.

- **Ecosystem Maturation:** The blockchain ecosystem has matured since the DAO hack, with improved tooling, security practices, and education. Developers now have more resources at their disposal to create secure smart contracts.

- **Bug Bounty Programs:** Many blockchain projects now offer bug bounty programs to incentivize researchers and developers to identify and report vulnerabilities in their code.

Despite these improvements, smart contract security remains challenging. As blockchain technology continues to evolve, so do the tactics and techniques of attackers. New vulnerabilities may emerge, and developers must remain vigilant in their efforts to protect smart contracts and the assets they control.

The Cybersecurity Opportunities in Blockchain

"Every disadvantage has its advantage."
– Johan Cruijff, Dutch professional football player and manager

It is not just in cryptocurrencies or NFTs that the specific characteristics of blockchain can be useful. Beyond these use cases, blockchain holds immense potential for cybersecurity.

- **Data Integrity and Authentication:** One of the fundamental problems in cybersecurity is ensuring the integrity of data. Blockchain technology can address this challenge by providing a tamper-proof ledger for critical information. Organizations can use blockchain to create immutable records of sensitive data, such as customer records, medical records, or intellectual property. This ensures that any unauthorized changes to the data are immediately detectable, enhancing trust and security.

- **Identity Management:** Identity theft and fraud are rampant. Blockchain can revolutionize identity management by creating a decentralized, secure system for verifying and managing identities. Users can have control over their personal information, granting permission for its use only when necessary. This reduces the risk of data breaches and identity theft.

- **Supply Chain Security:** Supply chain attacks pose a significant threat to businesses and governments alike. Blockchain can be used to enhance supply chain security by creating an immutable record of every step in the supply chain, from manufacturing to delivery. This transparency ensures that any attempts to tamper with the supply chain are easily detectable, reducing the risk of counterfeit products or malicious interference.

- **Incident Response and Forensics:** When a cybersecurity incident occurs, rapid response and thorough forensic analysis are crucial. Blockchain can be used to create an immutable record of incident response actions and forensic findings. This ensures that the investigation process is transparent and tamper-proof, essentially preserving the chain of custody.

- **Protection against DDoS Attacks:** Blockchain technology offers a multitude of cybersecurity opportunities. Its decentralized nature, transparency, and immutability make it a powerful tool for enhancing data integrity, identity management, supply chain security, incident response, and availability of data in the event of a DDoS attack.

As organizations and governments continue to struggle with evolving cyber threats, blockchain technology emerges as a promising tool to enhance cybersecurity.

Chapter 9

Biotechnology and Life Sciences: Unlocking Life's Code Securely

*"Technology could benefit or hurt people, so the usage of tech is
the responsibility of humanity as a whole, not just the discoverer."*
– Fei-Fei Li, professor of computer science at Stanford University

An Essential Overview of Biotechnology

"Biology is the most powerful technology ever created. DNA is software,
protein are hardware, cells are factories."
– Arvind Gupta, scientist

In December 2023, the use of clustered regularly interspaced short palindromic repeats (CRISPR) technology for treating sickle cell anemia was approved by the FDA in the USA. CRISPR is a revolutionary gene-editing technology, allowing scientists to precisely alter DNA sequences in living organisms. It is a revolutionary advancement in biotechnology, enabling targeted modifications at the genetic level. The collaborative effort between Vertex and CRISPR Therapeutics offered a functional cure by editing genes involved in red blood cell production. This revolutionary therapy involved editing the patient's bone marrow stem cells to produce healthy red blood cells, offering a potential lifelong cure. However, with a price tag of $2.2 million per patient, it remains inaccessible for most.

Biotechnology is the use of living systems and organisms to develop or improve products. It has rapidly grown in recent years, offering groundbreaking medical treatments, advancements in agriculture, environmental solutions, and more.

Another recent development is the use of CRISPR for cholesterol management. Starting in July 2022, advancements in CRISPR technology were utilized by Verve Therapeutics to develop a single-dose gene-editing medication for lowering cholesterol.

Biotechnology operates at the intersection of biology and technology, where the manipulation and harnessing of living organisms, systems, or processes contribute to advances in fields such as medicine, agriculture, and industry. Its impact is profound, touching many aspects of human life. From gene editing and personalized medicine to agricultural biotechnology and the development of biofuels, the transformative power of biotechnology promises to alleviate pressing global challenges and enhance human well-being.

Developments in precision medicine, where tailored treatments can be designed based on an individual's genetic makeup are becoming a reality. This capability has the potential to revolutionize the treatment of various diseases, offering more effective and personalized therapies that yield better patient outcomes. Biotechnology is driving breakthroughs in the development of novel vaccines, such as those designed to combat emerging infectious diseases, demonstrating its vital role in global health care.

In agriculture, biotechnological innovations have enabled the creation of genetically modified crops with enhanced nutritional content, improved resistance to pests and diseases, and greater tolerance to environmental stress. These advancements have the capacity to bolster food security, promote sustainable agriculture, and mitigate the adverse effects of climate change on crop yields. Biotechnology applications in agriculture also present opportunities to reduce reliance on harmful chemical pesticides, thereby safeguarding both human health and the environment. Some real-world examples include the use of genetic engineering to develop herbicide-resistant seeds for soybeans, genetically engineering apples with extended shelf life, and CRISPR gene edited cows that produce more milk.

Beyond health care and agriculture, biotechnology is reshaping industrial processes, driving the development of bio-based materials, renewable energy sources, and eco-friendly manufacturing techniques. Specifically, microorganisms and enzymes are being used to produce energy carriers such as biogas and bioethanol. From bioplastics, biofuels, and bioremediation solutions for environmental cleanup, the potential for biotechnology to foster sustainable practices and reduce the ecological footprint of various industries is vast. As society increasingly prioritizes environmental sustainability, biotechnology offers many solutions to current and future challenges.

The Role of Cybersecurity in Biotechnology

"In biology, nothing is clear, everything is too complicated, everything is a mess, and just when you think you understand something, you peel off a layer and find deeper complications beneath. Nature is anything but simple."
– Richard Preston, author of *The Hot Zone:*
The Terrifying True Story of the Origins of the Ebola Virus

In the closing months of 2023, a significant cybersecurity breach occurred at 23andMe, a leading personal genomics organization. This incident resulted in the unauthorized access and subsequent sale of private data belonging to millions of customers, on the dark web.

The attack appeared to be specifically targeted towards certain minority groups, who are frequently the victims of hate crimes. This incident underscores the vulnerability of the biotechnology industry to such cyber threats.

Cybersecurity serves as an enabler of biotechnology by safeguarding sensitive data, protecting intellectual property, ensuring regulatory compliance, and fostering a climate of trust and collaboration within the industry. By securing the digital infrastructure of biotechnology applications, cybersecurity plays a pivotal role in propelling advancements, securing sensitive information, and fostering an environment conducive to groundbreaking discoveries and life-changing innovations.

The industry's susceptibility to hacking can be attributed to a combination of two factors. Firstly, the nature of the data held by companies in this sector is highly sensitive and valuable, with the potential to cause significant harm to customers if misused. Secondly, the biotechnology industry has traditionally not been perceived as investing heavily in cybersecurity measures.

Some of the specific data privacy, ethics, and regulatory aspects worth considering include the following:

- **Safeguarding Sensitive Data:** One of the primary roles of cybersecurity in biotechnology is the safeguarding of sensitive data. The volume of sensitive data being generated and utilized is immense, including patient genetic information to proprietary research data. Cybersecurity controls ensure that this data remains confidential and inaccessible to unauthorized individuals or entities. Through encryption, secure data storage, and stringent access controls, cybersecurity creates a robust defense against data breaches, unauthorized access, and data manipulation.

- **Promoting Ethical Data Practices:** Ethical considerations play a crucial role in the biotechnology industry, especially concerning the handling of sensitive genetic information, human subject data, and experimental findings. Cybersecurity and data privacy promotes ethical data practices by ensuring the responsible and transparent management of sensitive data, respecting the privacy rights of individuals, and upholding the ethical standards set forth by regulatory bodies and industry associations. By implementing data anonymization techniques, consent management frameworks, and ethical data handling protocols, a culture of ethical data practices can be maintained.

- **Protecting Intellectual Property:** Intellectual property is the cornerstone of innovation and market competitiveness. Cybersecurity protects intellectual property, including research findings, experimental data, and proprietary algorithms, from cyber theft and industrial espionage. Nation states are an example of powerful adversaries targeting the biotechnology industry. Implementing robust authentication mechanisms and data encryption techniques ensures that the invaluable intellectual property of biotechnology advancements remains secure. This protection fosters an environment that encourages investment in research and development, thereby promoting continuous advancements and discoveries within the biotechnology sector.

- **Ensuring Regulatory Compliance:** Biotechnology often involves the handling of sensitive information and adherence to strict regulatory frameworks and compliance standards. Cybersecurity serves as a critical enabler in ensuring that biotechnological practices and research activities align with the stringent regulatory requirements imposed by governing bodies.

Some specific regulations of the biotechnology industry include:

- **European Commission's Biotechnology Regulations:** The European Commission has implemented a broad strategy and plan for the development of life sciences and biotechnology-based products.

- **Food and Drug Administration's Regulation of Plant and Animal Biotechnology Products:** The FDA regulates plant and animal biotechnology products in coordination with the US Department of Agriculture (USDA) and US Environmental Protection Agency (EPA), consistent with the US Coordinated Framework for the Regulation of Biotechnology (1984).

- **Regulation of Biotechnology under Toxic Substances Control Act (TSCA) and Federal Insecticide, Fungicide, and Rodenticide Act (FIFRA):** The US Environmental Protection Agency (EPA) regulates biotechnology under the TSCA and the FIFRA.

These regulations underscore the importance of compliance in the biotechnology sector, fostering public trust, and mitigating the risks associated with legal implications and penalties.

- **Fostering a Climate of Trust and Collaboration:** The complex nature of the biotechnology sector requires collaborative efforts among various stakeholders, including researchers, institutions, and industry players. Cybersecurity plays a pivotal role in fostering a climate of trust and collaboration by establishing secure communication channels and data-sharing platforms. Through the implementation of secure data exchange protocols and multi-layered authentication mechanisms, cybersecurity enables seamless collaboration while preserving the confidentiality and integrity of shared information. This climate of trust encourages knowledge sharing, promotes research partnerships, and accelerates the pace of innovation within the biotechnology sector.

By prioritizing robust cybersecurity measures, the biotechnology sector can continue to thrive, innovate, and make significant strides in revolutionizing health care, agriculture, and various other industries, all while maintaining the highest standards of security, ethics, and data integrity.

Securing the Era of Genomics and Personalized Medicine

"Genome design is going to be a key part of the future.
That's why we need fast, cheap, accurate DNA synthesis,
so you can make a lot of iterations of something and test them."
– Craig Venter, pioneer in genomics

In 2000, the estimated cost for generating an initial "draft" human genome sequence was approximately $300 million worldwide. This cost decreased significantly to about $14 million by 2006. By mid-2015, it dropped further to just above $4,000, and by late 2015, the costs had fallen below $1,500. As of 2022, depending on the country, the costs were around $300–$500. This example illustrates the rapid advancement of genomics and its increasing affordability for researchers, clinicians, and individuals.

Genomics is the study of an organism's complete set of DNA, including all of its genes. It involves analyzing and understanding the structure, function, evolution, and mapping of genomes, which are the entire genetic material of an organism. This field provides insights into how genes and genetic variations influence the biological characteristics and health of individuals.

Advances in genomics have allowed researchers to scan and compare entire genomes very quickly, revealing disease "signatures" for type 2 diabetes, heart disorders, prostate cancer, Crohn's disease, Parkinson's disease, and age-related macular degeneration. New disease-related gene variants are being continuously discovered.

Personalized medicine customizes treatment and healthcare strategies to the individual characteristics of each patient. It often relies on genetic information to guide the selection of the most effective treatments and preventative measures for specific diseases. This approach moves away from the current generic model, focusing instead on how individual genetic makeup can affect responses to medication, thereby optimizing patient care.

Among the first successful targeted therapies was the anticancer drug Imatinib, which is tailored to patients with chronic myelogenous leukemia (CML) who carry an enzyme called BCR-ABL tyrosine kinase, a protein produced by a cytogenetic abnormality known as the Philadelphia chromosome. Imatinib blocks the proliferation of CML cells that possess the mutated kinase, effectively reversing the abnormality's cancerous effects.

The remarkable advancements in genomics and personalized medicine have revolutionized health care, presenting extraordinary prospects for customized therapies and enhanced patient results. Alongside these advancements, a host of complex cybersecurity challenges has emerged, demanding protective measures to secure the sensitive data and ensure the integrity of this critical information.

The integration of genomics and personalized medicine presents unique cybersecurity challenges. One of the primary challenges lies in safeguarding the vast volumes of genomic data generated through sequencing technologies and personalized medical records. The confidential nature of this data, which includes highly sensitive genetic information and personalized health insights, makes it a prime target for cyber threats, ranging from data breaches and unauthorized access to targeted attacks aimed at manipulating genetic information, which could cost lives if exploited.

Securing genomic and personalized medical data involves addressing several key areas of concern. Data anonymization is a crucial process that safeguards individuals' privacy while preserving the inherent value of genomic data. Encryption plays a crucial role in protecting data during transmission and storage. Implementing robust encryption algorithms and mechanisms can significantly reduce the risk of unauthorized access and ensure that sensitive genomic information remains confidential.

The growing utilization of cloud-based storage and computing services in the field of genomics and personalized medicine introduces new security challenges. When leveraging cloud infrastructure for data storage and analysis, it is imperative to prioritize the selection of secure and reputable cloud service providers that offer robust security protocols, data encryption, and continuous monitoring to detect and mitigate potential threats. Additionally, performing regular backups are crucial to ensure data availability and resilience in the face of unexpected cyber incidents.

The evolving regulatory landscape surrounding data protection and privacy, such as the General Data Protection Regulation (GDPR) and the Health Insurance Portability and Accountability Act (HIPAA), requires strict adherence to compliance standards. Healthcare organizations and research institutions must ensure that their cybersecurity strategies align with these regulatory frameworks.

Securing the era of genomics and personalized medicine is essential for fostering patient trust and enabling the continued advancement of personalized healthcare services.

Ethical, Legal, and Cybersecurity Challenges in Biotechnology

"In the long history of humankind, those who learned to collaborate and improvise most effectively have prevailed."
— Charles Darwin, naturalist

In the biotechnology and life sciences industries, the convergence of science, technology, and ethics presents incredible opportunities and daunting challenges. As innovation accelerates and the boundaries of possibility expand, ethical frameworks and legal regulations are becoming increasingly important.

One of the interesting ethical quandaries surrounding biotechnology relates to human cloning. Human reproductive cloning, involving the creation of a genetic duplicate of a human being, is universally condemned due to the psychological, social, and physiological risks.

In 2007, researchers at Oregon Health & Science University's Oregon National Primate Research Center made a significant breakthrough in efforts to develop human stem cell therapies. This followed several previously unsuccessful attempts to clone a macaque, a type of primate. The method they used is called somatic cell nuclear transfer (SCNT), which involves transplanting the nucleus of the cell, containing an individual's DNA, to an egg cell that has had its genetic material removed. Despite numerous attempts, previous efforts to use the SCNT technology to clone stem cells in primates had repeatedly failed.

The team was able to extract stem cells from some of the cloned monkey embryos, persuading them to develop into mature heart and nerve cells in the laboratory. This breakthrough brought the possibility of cloning human embryos for use in research a step closer, raising the prospect of developing transplant tissues, to treat diseases such as diabetes and Parkinson's, that will not be rejected by the body.

In contrast, therapeutic cloning, which aims to produce embryonic stem cells for research and medical treatment, has divided opinions. While some view it as unethical, equating it to the creation and destruction of human life at the embryonic stage, others argue for its moral imperative in healing the sick and advancing scientific knowledge. Supporters of therapeutic cloning advocate for its funding and regulation, emphasizing the need for moral consideration of embryos, and caution against the exploitation of women and couples for their eggs or embryos.

These ethical controversies in biotechnology, particularly surrounding human cloning, highlight the complex interplay between scientific advancement and moral considerations, illustrating the need for careful ethical and legal frameworks to guide biotechnological innovations.

The Ethical Imperative

Biotechnology has the potential to transform human existence by providing innovative solutions to some of the most pressing challenges in health care, agriculture, and environmental conservation. This potential is naturally accompanied by many ethical dilemmas that cannot be ignored. One of the most prominent ethical considerations in biotechnology revolves around the question of what is morally acceptable when it comes to manipulating life at the genetic level.

The advent of CRISPR-Cas9 technology provides a striking ethical dilemma. This revolutionary gene-editing tool has raised profound questions about the boundaries of human intervention in the genetic code. In 2018, Chinese scientist He Jiankui shocked the world by announcing the birth of twin girls whose genes he had edited to make them resistant to HIV. The ethical implications of this experiment reverberated globally, leading to widespread condemnation and calls for stricter oversight.

Cybersecurity plays a crucial role in addressing these ethical concerns by ensuring that sensitive genetic data is protected from unauthorized access and tampering. As biotechnology researchers and companies handle vast amounts of very intimate genetic information, the safeguarding of this data becomes not only a legal requirement but also an ethical imperative.

The Legal Framework

Biotechnology operates within a complex web of legal regulations designed to strike a balance between fostering innovation and protecting public interest. The legal framework governing biotechnology varies from country to country but typically encompasses intellectual property rights, biosafety regulations, and ethical guidelines.

One notable regulatory development affecting the biotechnology industry is the European Union's General Data Protection Regulation (GDPR). Although primarily designed to protect personal data, GDPR also has implications for biotechnology, especially concerning the handling of genetic information. GDPR imposes strict requirements on how biotechnology organizations and research institutions collect, process, and store genetic data. Failure to comply can result in significant fines, making data privacy and cybersecurity measures a matter of legal compliance.

In the United States, the Genetic Information Nondiscrimination Act (GINA) prohibits discrimination in health coverage and employment based on genetic information. This legislation places additional legal obligations on organizations to safeguard genetic data.

The emergence of biotechnology patents and intellectual property disputes has created a legal battleground in which the rights to groundbreaking innovations are fiercely contested. The legal complexities surrounding biotechnology patents require companies to protect intellectual property and safeguard research and development data.

The Role of Cybersecurity

Cybersecurity ensures that there are adequate controls to protect sensitive genetic data, intellectual property, and responsible innovation.

In 2020, biotechnology organization Moderna, while developing the COVID-19 vaccine, became a target of cybercriminals seeking to steal valuable research data. Moderna's robust cybersecurity defenses thwarted the attack, ensuring that critical vaccine research remained secure. This incident is a chilling reminder of the importance of cybersecurity to safeguarding life-saving research from malicious actors.

Another example that emphasizes the symbiotic relationship between cybersecurity and biotechnology is the rise of bioinformatics. Bioinformatics helps analyze genetic data, making sense of the complex information encoded in genes. As biotechnology increasingly relies on computational analysis of genetic data, the protection of these datasets becomes crucial. Cybersecurity measures not only safeguard the integrity of genetic information but also ensure the accuracy of analyses and results, preventing erroneous conclusions that could have far-reaching consequences.

Balancing Act

The interplay between ethical, legal, and cybersecurity considerations in biotechnology is a delicate balancing act. On one hand, ethical principles guide in determining what is morally acceptable in manipulating life at the genetic level. On the other hand, legal frameworks establish the boundaries within which biotechnology can operate. In the biotechnology industry, cybersecurity serves as a crucial protective mechanism while also aiding further development.

Striking the right balance requires ongoing dialogue among stakeholders, including scientists, policymakers, ethicists, and cybersecurity experts. Past events, such as the global discussion following the CRISPR-Cas9 experiments in China and the legal battles over gene-editing patents, demonstrate the urgency of these discussions. Ultimately, our ability to harness the power of biotechnology relies on our ability to maintain a balance between ethics, legalities, and cybersecurity.

Future of Biotechnology: Cybersecurity Trends and Predictions

"The potential for synthetic biology and biotechnology is vast; we all have an opportunity to create the future together."
– Ryan Bethencourt, American Scientist

Biotechnology and life sciences have already made remarkable strides, transforming the way we understand, treat, and manipulate life itself. With the convergence of biology and technology, the possibilities appear limitless, from gene editing to personalized medicine. With these rapid advancements, it is worth exploring the future of biotechnology and the emerging cybersecurity trends and predictions that will shape this field.

Biotech companies and research institutions are pioneering innovation, often relying heavily on data-driven techniques and interconnected devices. This reliance on data and connectivity presents significant opportunities but also amplifies vulnerabilities that can be exploited by malicious actors.

In 2021, a group of researchers discovered vulnerabilities in the software used to control CRISPR gene-editing technology. This opened the door to potential cyberattacks on gene-editing processes, raising concerns about the integrity of genetic data and the potential for unauthorized gene edits.

During the COVID-19 pandemic, there were numerous reports of cyberattacks targeting organizations involved in vaccine research and development. State-sponsored actors were suspected of trying to steal critical research data and vaccine formulas, highlighting the geopolitical importance of biotech security.

To navigate the complex cybersecurity landscape of biotechnology effectively, it is crucial for industry leaders and researchers to stay ahead of the curve. Here are some emerging cybersecurity trends to watch:

- **Quantum Encryption:** As quantum computing matures, it poses a significant threat to traditional encryption methods. Biotech companies will need to adopt quantum-resistant encryption techniques to safeguard sensitive genetic data and research findings.

- **Secure Supply Chains:** The biotech industry relies on a global network of suppliers. Strengthening the cybersecurity of this supply chain is essential to prevent tampering or counterfeiting of critical biotech materials.

- **IoT Security:** IoT has made its way into biotech labs, facilitating remote monitoring and data collection. However, IoT devices are often vulnerable to cyberattacks. Robust IoT security measures will be vital to protect lab equipment and experimental data.

- **Privacy Preservation:** As genomics and personalized medicine become more prevalent, protecting the privacy of individuals' genetic data will be crucial. Advanced encryption and data anonymization techniques will be needed to ensure data privacy and compliance with regulations like GDPR and HIPAA.

- **Threat Intelligence Sharing:** Collaboration among biotech organizations, research institutions, and cybersecurity experts is essential for staying informed about emerging threats. Threat intelligence sharing platforms will become more prevalent, enabling timely responses to cyber threats.

Predictions for the Future

Several cybersecurity predictions emerge for the biotechnology and life sciences sector:

- **Increased Ransomware Attacks:** Cybercriminals will continue to target biotechnology organizations with ransomware attacks, aiming to disrupt research and extort funds. Organizations must invest in robust backup systems, employee training, and incident response plans to mitigate these threats.

- **Regulatory Scrutiny:** Governments worldwide will place greater emphasis on cybersecurity regulations specific to the biotechnology industry. Organizations will face stricter compliance requirements and penalties for data breaches.

- **Biotechnology Espionage:** Nation-state actors will intensify their efforts to steal biotechnology research data for economic, political, and military advantage. International cooperation will be essential to combat these threats effectively.

- **Insider Threats:** Insider threats will persist as employees with access to valuable biotechnology data may be tempted to compromise security. Continuous monitoring and user behavior analytics will help detect and prevent such threats.

- **Ethical Hacking:** Biotechnology organizations will increasingly engage ethical hackers to identify and address vulnerabilities proactively. Bug bounty programs and security audits will become common practice.

As biotechnology continues to advance, it is crucial for leaders and professionals in the field to recognize that cybersecurity is not a secondary concern but an integral part of research and development. Recent incidents, such as the CRISPR hack and COVID-19 research espionage, serve as reminders of the vulnerabilities that exist in the biotechnology industry.

To secure the future of biotechnology, it is imperative that organizations prioritize cybersecurity as an essential component of their operations.

Chapter 10

Exploring Additional
Emerging Technologies

"You may not be able to alter reality, but you can alter your attitude towards it, and this, paradoxically, alters reality. Try it and see."
– Margaret Atwood, Author

10

Health Technology:
Cybersecurity in the Digital Healthcare Era

*"If you zoom out into the future, and you look back, and you ask the question, '
What was Apple's greatest contribution to mankind?' it will be about health."*
— Tim Cook, CEO Apple Inc.

In November 2023, Forward Health launched CarePods, a self-contained, AI-powered doctor's office. The CarePods blend AI with medical expertise to create immersive experiences, putting patients in control of their health.

Key features of the CarePods included advanced diagnostics and personalized health plans; a broad range of health apps designed to treat current issues and prevent future ones; on-demand access to services like disease detection, biometric body scans, and blood testing; and deployment in accessible locations like malls, gyms, and offices.

The health apps were built by Forward's team of doctors from top universities like Harvard, Johns Hopkins, and Columbia. These apps address a wide range of disease areas, including diabetes, hypertension, depression, and anxiety. Data from CarePod visits are securely transmitted to Forward's platform, enabling continuous progress monitoring, identifying disease risks, and providing in-depth evaluations using sensors, laboratory tests, and vital sign measurements.

The intersection of health care and technology has revolutionized health care advancements. The once-clear boundaries between medical devices and everyday technology are increasingly blurred, as demonstrated by developments like Forward's CarePod and wearable technologies like the Apple Watch, which serves additionally as a fitness tracker and a health monitoring tool.

The ongoing digital transformation of the medical industry, also known as the Internet of Medical Things (IoMT), refers to a connected infrastructure of medical devices, software applications, health systems, and services that use networking technologies to communicate and exchange data with each other and with other healthcare IT systems. The variety of some key IoMT devices and technologies is impressive.

- **Wearable Health Monitors:** Devices like smartwatches, fitness trackers, and heart rate monitors collect various health metrics such as heart rate, blood pressure, and activity levels, transmitting this data to healthcare providers for monitoring and analysis.

- **Remote Patient Monitoring (RPM) Devices:** These include blood glucose monitors, cardiac monitors, and respiratory monitors that enable the remote collection and transmission of patient data. RPM is particularly useful for chronic disease management and post-operative care.

- **Smart Implants:** These are devices like pacemakers, cochlear implants, and drug delivery systems that are implanted into the patient's body. They not only perform their therapeutic functions but also collect and transmit data about patient health.

- **Connected Inhalers and Insulin Pumps:** These devices are used for conditions like asthma and diabetes. They monitor usage, dosage, and provide reminders, improving adherence to medication schedules and treatment effectiveness.

- **Telemedicine Devices:** This includes digital stethoscopes, otoscopes, and dermascopes that enable remote consultations. They capture medical data and transmit it to healthcare professionals for diagnosis and treatment.

- **Hospital Bed Sensors:** Smart beds, equipped with sensors that monitor patient vitals, movements, and weight, assist in patient care management, ensuring timely interventions and reducing the risk of pressure ulcers.

- **Smart Home Health Monitors:** Devices integrated into a patient's home, such as fall detectors, motion sensors, and bed exit sensors, provide real-time data to caregivers about the patient's daily activities and alert them in case of emergencies.

- **Mobile Health Applications:** Smartphone apps that collect health data and provide health-related services range from fitness tracking to medication reminders and mental health support.

- **Virtual Health Assistants:** AI-powered virtual assistants are used in patient engagement, reminding patients to take medications, follow treatment plans, or schedule appointments.

To adequately protect the Internet of Medical Things (IoMT) technologies, several cybersecurity measures should be implemented. These measures not only ensure the security and integrity of the devices and the data they handle, but they also safeguard patient privacy and compliance with regulatory standards. Unsurprisingly, many of the already established cybersecurity controls are essential to IoMT technologies and environments.

Specific cybersecurity measures that should be taken for IoMT technologies include:

- **Education and Training:** Regular training and awareness programs for healthcare staff and patients about cybersecurity best practices, common threats like phishing, and safe device usage are crucial.

- **Secure Device Configuration and Management:** Ensuring that IoMT devices are securely configured and properly managed throughout their lifecycle, including safe decommissioning, is crucial to prevent security loopholes and patient privacy.

- **Device and User Behavior Analytics:** Leveraging analytics to understand normal device and user behaviors can help in quickly identifying anomalies that may indicate a cyber threat.

- **Incident Response Plan:** Having a well-defined and regularly tested incident response plan ensures that organizations are prepared to respond to and recover from cyber incidents. Incidents should be communicated to patients quickly and clearly should the need arise.

Customized cybersecurity frameworks are also emerging, tailored to the specific needs and risks of individual healthcare providers. These frameworks consider the unique nature of healthcare data and operations, offering a more focused approach to cybersecurity. For example, the Health Sector Coordinating Council Cybersecurity Working Group and the U.S. Department of Health and Human Services jointly released a guide to help the public and private healthcare sectors align their cybersecurity programs with the NIST Cybersecurity Framework. This guide provides specific steps that healthcare organizations can take to manage cyber risks to their information technology systems and reduce the number of cyber incidents affecting the sector.

There are a few healthcare-specific security standards and regulations that need to be adhered to, such as HIPAA in the US, and GDPR in Europe. These existing regulations will aid in ensuring that advances in the medical field are executed in a responsible manner.

The integration of IoMT into health care represents a significant advancement in medical technology. These advancements require healthcare providers to protect sensitive patient data, maintain device integrity, and ensure the continuity of care.

Cybersecurity in Additive Manufacturing and 3D Printing

"3D printing will massively reduce the cost of certain products as the cost of labor is removed."
– Peter Diamandis, founder of Singularity University

3D printing has gained popularity among many individuals, particularly using consumer-grade home printers. These innovative devices can produce a wide range of objects, including toys and household items. However, 3D printing has evolved significantly in recent years and is now being used for much more complex purposes such as manufacturing aerospace components, medical devices, and even entire buildings. In health care, items like tooth implants, heart valves, and knee replacements can all be 3D printed. Currently in development, entire organs could be 3D printed, which could dramatically improve outcomes for patients awaiting transplants. In the food industry, 3D printing is being used to create food items with complex shapes and designs. Sweets and chocolates were among the first foods to be 3D printed, but the technology has grown to include basic pizzas, various sauces, pasta, and even cruelty-free meat and sushi.

However, as with any technology deeply integrated with digital processes, 3D printing faces significant cybersecurity risks. Intellectual property theft, product tampering, and the potential for sabotaging supply chain and manufacturing processes are some of the cybersecurity concerns affecting 3D printing.

Intellectual Property Theft

Intellectual property (IP) is the lifeblood of additive manufacturing, where unique digital designs represent significant investments in research and development. The digitization of these designs, however, makes them vulnerable to theft and unauthorized replication. Cybercriminals can breach network security to steal these files, leading to loss of competitive advantage and financial damage. This issue is exacerbated in industries where design intricacies equate to substantial intellectual and monetary value, such as in aerospace or biomedical device manufacturing. The theft of IP not only impacts revenue but can also damage a company's market position and lead to legal complications if proprietary designs are replicated and sold by others.

Product Tampering

Product tampering in 3D printing, through data integrity attacks, involves unauthorized alterations to digital design files or printer settings. Such tampering can result in the production of defective or substandard products, with potentially disastrous consequences. In sectors like automotive or aerospace, where precision and reliability are paramount, compromised part integrity can lead to catastrophic failures and endanger lives. Beyond physical safety risks, these attacks can erode customer trust and tarnish brand reputation. Data integrity issues may not be immediately apparent, making them particularly insidious and hard to trace back to the source of tampering.

Supply Chain Risks

The distributed nature of 3D printing, particularly when integrated into global supply chains, introduces multiple points of vulnerability. The process often involves various stakeholders, from design teams and material suppliers to manufacturing units and delivery services. Each node in this chain is a potential target for cyberattacks, capable of disrupting operations. Cybercriminals may intercept communications, manipulate logistics data, or introduce counterfeit materials into the production process. Such vulnerabilities demand stringent cybersecurity measures across the entire supply chain, emphasizing the protection of data and the verification of the integrity and origin of physical materials and components used in the printing process.

Industrial Espionage

Industrial espionage in the context of additive manufacturing involves competitors or malicious entities engaging in covert activities to steal or sabotage sensitive manufacturing data. This can range from hacking into an organization's network to gather trade secrets, to planting insiders within the organization to leak information. The competitive nature of industries leveraging 3D printing technology makes them prime targets for such espionage activities. The ramifications extend beyond immediate financial losses. They can lead to long-term setbacks in research and development, loss of market share, and irreversible damage to a company's reputation. It is crucial for organizations to implement advanced surveillance and monitoring systems, coupled with stringent access controls and employee vetting procedures, to mitigate the risks associated with industrial espionage.

Cybersecurity Measures

Specific cybersecurity measures in additive manufacturing involve securing digital files and rigorous supply chain security. Securing digital files is a crucial step in protecting intellectual property and ensuring the integrity of 3D printed products. Encryption is a primary defense mechanism, rendering the design files unreadable to unauthorized users, protecting files at rest (when stored) and in transit (when sent over networks). Digital watermarking and fingerprinting of files can be employed to trace the origin and verify the authenticity of the designs, deterring IP theft and enabling tracking in case of a breach.

Securing the additive manufacturing supply chain requires a multi-faceted approach, similar to other complex industries. It starts with thorough vetting of suppliers and partners, ensuring they have robust cybersecurity measures in place. Establishing secure communication channels between supply chain partners is important. Implementing blockchain technology could offer a more secure and transparent way to track the movement and origin of materials and components, ensuring their authenticity.

As additive manufacturing technology evolves, it is likely to see advancements in printing speed, material diversity, and the complexity of printable designs. These advancements, while beneficial, may also introduce new cybersecurity vulnerabilities. As 3D printing becomes more integrated with other emerging technologies like AI and IoT, there will be a need for comprehensive security strategies that address the interconnected nature of these systems. Future threats might also include more sophisticated forms of IP theft, such as AI-driven reverse engineering of printed products. By staying ahead of these trends, organizations can better prepare and protect themselves against the next generation of cybersecurity challenges in additive manufacturing.

Advanced Materials and Nanotechnology: Securing the Building Blocks of the Future

"Nanotechnology is the idea that we can create devices and machines all the way down to the nanometer scale, which is a billionth of a meter, about half the width of a human DNA molecule."
— Paul McEuen, professor of physics at Cornell University

Imagine a world where materials are not only stronger and lighter but also more adaptable, and more durable than what we have traditionally used. This is the world of advanced materials. Moving beyond conventional materials like steel and plastic, advanced materials encompass a broad range of substances, each engineered to offer exceptional qualities. They include ceramics that can withstand extreme temperatures, polymers that change shape upon electrical stimulation, and composites that blend different materials to achieve superior strength and lightness. These materials are revolutionizing industries like aerospace, where the demand for lighter yet stronger materials is crucial for fuel efficiency and performance. In the automotive industry, they contribute to safer and more efficient vehicles, while in electronics, they enable smaller, faster, and more powerful devices.

The creation of advanced materials involves sophisticated techniques that manipulate their composition, structure, and properties to achieve desired performance characteristics.

- **Composite Material Fabrication**: This involves combining two or more distinct materials to create a new material with enhanced properties. For instance, carbon fiber composites are made by embedding carbon fibers in a polymer matrix, resulting in materials that are strong yet lightweight. The process can involve techniques like molding, where the materials are shaped and cured under heat and pressure.

- **Alloy Development:** Advanced alloys, like those used in aerospace, are created by melting and mixing different metals in specific proportions. This process, known as alloying, involves careful temperature control and often includes subsequent treatments like annealing (heating and then cooling) to improve the material's strength and durability.

- **Nanomaterial Synthesis:** Advanced materials often incorporate nanoscale structures. These are typically created through chemical or physical processes that build the material atom by atom or molecule by molecule. Techniques like chemical vapor deposition (CVD) or sol-gel processing are common for creating thin films or coatings with nanoscale precision.

Nanotechnology operates on the nanoscale, where a nanometer is one-billionth of a meter. To put this into perspective, a single human hair is about 80,000 to 100,000 nanometers wide. At this tiny scale, materials exhibit properties that do not exist at larger scales, opening a world of possibilities. Nanotechnology involves manipulating matter at the atomic or molecular level to create new materials and devices. This could mean making materials more resistant to heat, improving the delivery of drugs in the body, or even developing nanoscale sensors for environmental monitoring.

The global market for nanotechnology, expected to reach $125 billion by 2024, is a testament to its growing influence. In November 2023, Google's DeepMind developed a deep learning tool called Graph Networks for Materials Exploration (GNoME), which led to the discovery of 2.2 million new crystals. These theoretically stable but experimentally unrealized combinations are equivalent to nearly 800 years' worth of knowledge or 45 times more than discovered previously.

Advanced materials and nanotechnology, being at the forefront of scientific innovation, present unique cybersecurity challenges. These challenges are a blend of highly technical risks and broader concerns about data integrity and intellectual property. Some of the notable cybersecurity issues in this field include the following:

- **Manipulation of Research Data:** Cyberattackers could manipulate research data or experimental results, leading to incorrect conclusions or unsafe applications of materials and technologies. This could have severe implications for industries relying on this research, like pharmaceuticals, aerospace, and electronics.

- **Complexity of Nanoscale Devices:** As devices and materials become smaller and more complex, securing them against tampering or unauthorized access becomes more challenging. Nanoscale devices might be used in critical applications, making them attractive targets for sabotage.

- **R&D Espionage:** Research and development in advanced materials and nanotechnology are highly competitive fields. Industrial espionage, including cyber espionage, is a significant threat, as competitors or nation states may seek to gain a technological advantage.

- **Data Intensive Processes:** Nanotechnology and advanced materials research and development are data intensive. Managing and securing large volumes of data, often sensitive or proprietary, poses a challenge, particularly against threats like ransomware or data breaches.

- **Intellectual Property Theft:** Advanced materials and nanotechnologies often represent cutting-edge research and significant investments. The theft of intellectual property (such as research data, manufacturing processes, or chemical formulas) is a major concern, as it can lead to significant economic and competitive losses.

- **Regulatory Compliance:** The field of advanced materials and nanotechnology is subject to various regulations, including export controls and safety standards. Ensuring cybersecurity compliance with these regulations is crucial but challenging due to the evolving nature of both the technology and the regulatory landscape.

As nanotechnology continues to advance, robust cybersecurity measures will be crucial in protecting the integrity of research and ensuring that the transformative potential of these advanced materials is realized.

FinTech: Cybersecurity in the Financial Future

"Fintech is not a buzzword; it's the future of finance."
— Chris Skinner, strategist and author

The financial industry is undergoing a significant transformation and disruption. The advent of financial technology, commonly known as fintech, marks a paradigm shift in how financial services are rendered and consumed.

Fintech refers to the integration of technology into offerings by financial services companies to improve their use and delivery to consumers. It primarily works by unbundling services offered by traditional financial institutions and creating new markets for them. Fintech includes a broad spectrum of technologies and innovations applied to personal and commercial finance. This includes things like:

- **Digital Payments and Transfers:** Services that allow for the electronic exchange of money, such as mobile payment apps and peer-to-peer transfer services.

- **Blockchain and Cryptocurrencies:** The use of blockchain technology for financial transactions and the creation and management of digital currencies like Bitcoin.

- **Robo-Advising and Stock-Trading Apps:** Automated, algorithm-driven financial planning services with little to no human supervision, and platforms that allow individual investors to trade stocks and other securities.

- **Peer-to-Peer Lending and Crowdfunding:** Platforms that allow individuals to lend to or invest in others directly without the use of a traditional financial institution as an intermediary.

- **Insurtech:** The use of technology to disrupt and improve the insurance industry.

- **RegTech:** Technologies that help financial service firms comply with regulations.

The objective of fintech is to make financial services more accessible, faster, and cost-effective, often leveraging mobile connectivity, big data, and advanced analytics. Fintech has also been a driving force in the democratization of financial services, making tools and services that were once only available to the affluent or institutions accessible to a broader audience (previously unbanked).

The fintech sector, with its innovative approach to banking and investment, is reshaping the financial landscape. By 2025, the global fintech market is expected to reach $305 billion, reflecting its increasing impact. This growth makes fintech a prime target for cybercriminals. Data breaches, identity theft, and financial fraud are just some of the threats that these companies must protect against.

Robust cybersecurity measures are a fundamental aspect for maintaining customer trust and a regulatory requirement. This is well established even in traditional finance. John Reed, the CEO of Citibank, who created the first CISO position back in the 1990s, famously said, *"Citibank sells two things: money and trust. And without the trust, you can't sell the money."* A security breach of a fintech organization can have repercussions that extend beyond only financial losses. It can cause a significant erosion of customer confidence, which is particularly devastating in an industry that relies heavily on trust. In August 2021, hackers exploited a vulnerability in Poly Network. The aim of this platform is to establish connections between diverse blockchains, enabling seamless collaboration and cooperation among them. Hackers stole more than $600 million worth of cryptocurrency.

Clearly, the fintech industry inherently faces a unique set of cybersecurity challenges due to its digital nature and the sensitive financial data it handles. Some key cybersecurity challenges specific to the fintech sector include:

- **Data Security and Privacy:** FinTech companies deal with large volumes of sensitive financial data, making data security and privacy paramount. It is vital to protect against data breaches, ensure data integrity, and comply with data protection regulations like GDPR. Breaches in this sector can have devastating consequences, from financial losses for individuals and institutions to eroded trust in the financial system at large. As an example, in September 2022, Revolut, a financial technology company best known for its banking app, suffered a data breach that affected 50,000 customers worldwide.

- **Mobile and App-Based Vulnerabilities:** Many fintech services are delivered through mobile apps, which can have unique vulnerabilities. Ensuring the security of these apps against hacking, eavesdropping, and malware is a significant challenge.

- **API and Third-Party Integration Risks:** Fintech firms often rely on APIs and third-party integrations for services like payment gateways, data analytics, and cloud storage. Securing these integrations and ensuring the third parties also adhere to stringent cybersecurity measures is crucial.

- **Advanced Persistent Threats (APTs):** Fintech companies, due to their financial nature, are attractive targets for APTs. These are sophisticated, continuous cyberattacks, often state-sponsored or by organized crime groups, aimed at stealing financial data or disrupting financial services.

- **Compliance with Financial Regulations:** The financial sector is heavily regulated. Fintech companies must navigate and comply with a complex web of financial regulations, including cybersecurity standards, which can vary significantly across different jurisdictions.

- **Insider Threats:** Whether intentional or accidental, actions by employees can pose significant security risks. Managing insider threats requires a combination of robust security protocols, employee training, and monitoring systems.

- **Blockchain and Cryptocurrency-Related Risks:** Many fintech companies use blockchain and cryptocurrencies. These technologies pose unique challenges, such as securing crypto wallets, protecting against blockchain-specific vulnerabilities, and managing the regulatory uncertainty around cryptocurrencies.

- **Fraud and Identity Theft:** As digital financial services grow, so do incidents of online fraud and identity theft. Fintech firms must implement sophisticated fraud detection and prevention mechanisms to protect their customers.

Fintech organizations need to continue to invest heavily in cybersecurity to ensure the success of the industry. These challenges can be addressed with a proactive, multi-layered cybersecurity strategy that includes advanced technological solutions, regular security training for employees, strict compliance with regulatory requirements, and continuous monitoring and updating of security protocols. Organizations are also exploring innovative approaches like behavioral analytics and artificial intelligence to detect and prevent fraudulent activities.

The Final Frontier: Cybersecurity Considerations in Space Exploration

"For us to have a future that's exciting and inspiring,
it has to be one where we're a space-bearing civilization."
— Elon Musk, Tesla and SpaceX CEO

The space industry has evolved from being government-led to including significant contributions from private companies. The industry encompasses a wide range of activities, including satellite manufacturing, ground support equipment, and launch capabilities. The advent of private space travel has opened new opportunities and challenges, marking the beginning of the commercial space age. The US is the main driver of the global space economy's growth, which is projected to grow to $1 trillion by 2030.

The need to secure the technology that drives space exploration has become increasingly vital. There are national and economic security concerns regarding the threats to space innovation. These include harming corporate reputations by foreign entities creating counterfeit products, siphoning intellectual property, collecting sensitive data, and even going as far as to disrupt satellite communications.

One striking example of the vulnerabilities faced in the space sector occurred in 1998, when hackers took control of the German-US ROSAT satellite. Hackers commanded the satellite to turn its solar panels directly towards the sun, permanently damaging the satellite and rendering it useless. This incident resulted in a loss of millions of dollars and was a wake-up call to the global space community about the tangible threats of cyberattacks in space. It underscored the importance of robust cybersecurity measures in protecting valuable space assets and the sensitive data they handle. This event, though unfortunate, played a pivotal role in shaping current cybersecurity strategies in space exploration and satellite communication.

Ground Stations and Launch Facilities on Earth

Ground stations and launch facilities are pivotal for space missions. Ground stations are advanced, high-tech communication centers on Earth. They are equipped with large antennas and other communication equipment to send and receive signals to and from satellites or spacecraft in space. This communication can include sending commands to the spacecraft, receiving data like images or scientific information, and tracking the location of satellites.

Launch facilities are specialized sites where spacecraft, such as rockets and shuttles, are assembled, tested, and launched into space. They have structures like launch pads, control centers, and vehicle assembly buildings. These facilities are responsible for the safe and precise launch of spacecraft. They ensure that the spacecraft are correctly positioned, fueled, and ready for the journey into space.

Ground stations and launch facilities are susceptible to both physical and cyberattacks. Cybersecurity here involves safeguarding against hacking, espionage, and sabotage.

These facilities handle sensitive data including mission parameters, satellite control codes, and telemetry data. Ensuring the integrity and confidentiality of this data is crucial to prevent unauthorized access and manipulation.

Ground-to-Space Communications

Communications between Earth and spacecrafts are crucial for space missions. They involve advanced technologies for secure data transmission, including robust encryption and specialized communication protocols. These technologies are essential to protect against interception and unauthorized access, ensuring that only authorized commands are sent, and sensitive data is received securely.

Ground-to-space communication systems are also equipped to counter threats like signal jamming and interference. Technologies with multi-frequency/multi-system receivers and anti-jamming capabilities are used to reinforce the resilience of navigation systems to interference. This is critical for maintaining control over space assets. Ensuring uninterrupted and secure communication is vital for the success of missions, as it allows for real-time command, control, and receipt of valuable data from spacecraft.

Securing these communications involves not just technological solutions but also adherence to strict cybersecurity protocols. This ensures the integrity of transmitted data and the operational functionality of space assets, which is essential to space exploration and satellite operations.

In-Space Assets (Satellites, Spacecraft)

Satellites and spacecraft, integral to modern space missions, are equipped with sophisticated onboard computer systems. These systems implement the satellite's vital functions, such as attitude and orbit control, telecommand execution or dispatching, housekeeping telemetry gathering and formatting, onboard time synchronization and distribution, failure detection, isolation, recovery, etc.

Since these assets are controlled remotely, the security of command-and-control links is paramount. Ensuring these links are secure is essential to prevent unauthorized access or potential hijacking. This involves advanced encryption methods and continuous monitoring and updating of security protocols to safeguard these vital communications. The specifics of these technologies and protocols can vary depending on the mission and the organizations involved.

Cross-Constellation Communications

In satellite constellations, inter-satellite links, also known as "crosslinking," play a vital role. These links facilitate data exchange within the constellation, making their protection crucial for maintaining data integrity. Secure communication protocols and encryption are key to safeguarding these links from cyber threats. Techniques that generate encryption keys based on properties or features directly associated with the actual satellites are being explored, removing the necessity for key storage.

Resilience against space weather effects is essential. Satellite communications can be impacted by natural phenomena like solar flares. Space weather can lead to a total loss of communication due to attenuation and/or severe scintillation when the broadcast signals cross the ionosphere. Building robust systems that can withstand both space weather and cyber threats is important for the reliability and security of satellite operations.

Evidently, cybersecurity challenges in the space industry are distinct and complex, arising from the unique environment and high-stakes nature of space operations. Some of the key cybersecurity challenges include the following:

- **Long-Distance Communication Delays:** Communication between Earth and spacecraft can experience significant delays, especially for missions far from Earth (like Mars missions). This delay makes real-time monitoring and response to cyber threats challenging.

- **Harsh Space Environment:** Spacecraft and satellites operate in extreme conditions, including intense radiation and varying temperatures. This environment can affect the reliability of onboard computing systems and increase vulnerability to cyberattacks.

- **Limited Physical Access for Repair:** Once a spacecraft is launched, physical access for maintenance or repair is extremely limited, if not impossible. Thus, any cybersecurity measures must be robust from the start, as updates and fixes are difficult to implement.

- **Sophisticated Attacks on Satellite Systems:** Satellites are critical infrastructure for global communications, navigation, and observation. They can be targets for sophisticated cyberattacks aimed at intercepting, jamming, or corrupting data streams.

- **Cross-Constellation Communication Risks:** As more satellites are launched, forming constellations for global coverage (like GPS or internet satellites), the risk of a single compromised satellite affecting others increases. Ensuring secure communication within these constellations is a challenge.

- **Dependency on Ground Stations:** Ground stations, vital for controlling and communicating with space assets, can be targets of cyberattacks. Compromising a ground station can lead to unauthorized control or disruption of space assets.

- **Supply Chain Vulnerabilities:** Space missions involve complex supply chains with multiple vendors. Each component in the supply chain, from software providers to hardware manufacturers, can introduce vulnerabilities.

- **International Collaboration and Data Sharing:** Space missions often involve collaboration between different countries and companies. This cooperation requires sharing sensitive data, which can pose security risks if not properly managed.

- **Regulatory and Jurisdictional Challenges:** Space operations often transcend national borders, leading to jurisdictional challenges in implementing and enforcing cybersecurity measures.

Cybersecurity Frameworks: There are several cybersecurity frameworks specific to space missions:

- The U.S. Department of State has released a framework to promote the US policy on cybersecurity and Information and Communications Technologies (ICTS) in space.

- The Consultative Committee for Space Data Systems (CCSDS) has published a report titled "Security Threats Against Space Missions," which presents an overview of threats against space missions.

- The National Institute of Standards and Technology (NIST) has published the final version of its guidance on applying the Cybersecurity Framework to the ground segment of space operations.

- The Federal Register has published a document titled "Cybersecurity Principles for Space Systems," which outlines guiding principles for cybersecurity.

These frameworks provide guidelines and best practices for ensuring the security of space missions. The specifics of these frameworks can vary depending on the mission and the organizations involved. It is important to note that cybersecurity in space is a rapidly evolving field, and new frameworks and guidelines are likely to be developed as technology advances and new threats emerge. For example, the IEEE Standards Association has established a Space Systems Cybersecurity Working Group to define a standard of cybersecurity controls for space systems, including modules for the ground systems, space vehicles, link segments, and the integration layer.

As humanity continues to push the boundaries of space exploration, it is crucial to expand cybersecurity measures accordingly. Protecting the technologies that drive space exploration is a fundamental necessity and a matter of national security.

Towards a Secure Future with Disruptive Technologies

"The past, like the future, is indefinite
and exists only as a spectrum of possibilities."
— Stephen Hawking, theoretical physicist

As this book draws to a close, it weaves together the lessons learned from the exploration of various disruptive technologies, highlighting the paramount role of cybersecurity in ensuring a safe and secure future, and emphasizing how cybersecurity is not just a safeguard but a fundamental enabler of growth and success of these innovations.

There is a symbiotic relationship between technological advancement and cybersecurity. In a time full of potential, the strategic integration of robust cybersecurity measures is crucial for the successful adoption and implementation of these technologies.

"Innovation is the ability to see change as an opportunity, not a threat."
— Steve Jobs, founder of Apple

Manifesto for Innovative Technology Leaders:
Pioneering Secure and Responsible Technology

1. **Prioritize Security and Privacy by Design:** As innovators in technology, you commit to making security and privacy a foundational element, not an afterthought. You understand that robust security measures and privacy are integral to the trust and functionality of our technologies.

2. **Champion Ethical Innovation:** You pursue innovation responsibly. Your advancements will respect privacy, uphold ethical standards, and contribute positively to society. You recognize that technology should be a force for good, empowering and uplifting, rather than exploiting or marginalizing.

3. **Embrace Transparency:** You vow to be transparent concerning data usage and the security of your solutions. You will clearly communicate your methods and intentions to users, fostering trust and accountability.

4. **Foster Inclusivity and Diversity:** In your pursuit of technological advancements, you will ensure inclusivity and diversity in your teams, your approach, and in your technology. You believe that a diverse range of perspectives leads to more robust, universally beneficial technologies.

5. **Commit to Continuous Learning:** The landscape of technology and cybersecurity is ever evolving. You commit to continuous learning and adaptation, ensuring your teams and technologies remain at the forefront of innovation and security.

6. **Collaborate for a Safer Digital World:** You acknowledge that no company operates in isolation. You will collaborate with peers, governments, and international bodies to advance secure, ethical, and responsible tech practices worldwide.

7. **Prepare for the Future:** You commit to forward-thinking, anticipating future challenges and opportunities in cybersecurity. You will develop technologies that not only meet today's needs but are also resilient and adaptable to the challenges of tomorrow.

8. **Promote User Empowerment and Education:** You believe in empowering users with the knowledge and tools to use technology safely. You will invest in user education and support, ensuring that your products enhance, rather than complicate, the user experience.

9. **Uphold Accountability:** You will hold yourself accountable for the impact of our technologies. You pledge to monitor, review, and

continually improve your practices, remaining vigilant against potential abuses or unforeseen consequences.

10. **Lead with Vision and Integrity:** Above all, you will lead with a clear vision and integrity, setting a standard for what it means to be at the forefront of technology. You will build not just for today but for a sustainable, secure, and responsible tomorrow.

....**and remember, technology has never evolved as rapidly as now, and it will never again be this slow.**

Acknowledgements

Tiago's Acknowledgments: I could not have written this without the unconditional love of my family. Ana, Inês, and Rita, you are one of a kind. I am so happy to have you in my life. I am lost for words for how proud I am of you. You are funny, caring, loving, and kind, with a heart as warm as your wit is sharp, making every moment spent in your company an absolute delight. Ana, you have put your career on pause in support of mine and I am eternally grateful to you for everything you are, everything you have done for our daughters, and for everything you have done for me.

To my fellow writer, Arnaud, I am thankful for your invitation to go on this crazy journey to write a book together. It was a lot of fun! There was never a dull moment, and it was always an exciting journey!

To Martijn Dekker for your outstanding inspirational leadership over the years. Thank you so much for everything you have done for the protection of organizations, their clients, and society. Your acceptance to write the foreword to this book is a delicate touch of kindness.

To my mother and father, I am eternally grateful for your unconditional supporting love and for teaching me all the values I carry. Thank you also to my siblings Bruno and Vanessa. So much of who I am is shaped by who you are.

For bonuses go to ...

To Noor Spanjaard, I am thankful for your tireless, caring love and attention. In the toughest times, you were always there for me. I learn a lot from you every day. You make the world around you better.

To João Pequenão, I am thankful for pioneering in my close group of friends this crazy concept of writing a book. Thank you also for so many open-minded, late-night talks. Your creative brain is one of a kind.

To Theo Hegeman, I am thankful for your tremendous open heart and your willingness to help everyone around you. Kindness is contagious. Thoughtfulness is rare. You possess both, in abundance.

To all my extended family, I am thankful for your love and support. It takes a village.

I am very lucky to have had outstanding colleagues across industries and countries who inspire me every day. Jenny Gershkovich, your sheer audacity inspires me to want more, do more, and reach for more. Malou van den Berg, thank you for showing me the power of being my full self—the world needs more people like you. Coen Klaver, thank you for believing in me and giving me my first management role. You are an amazing source of inspiration in everything you do.

To Rob Havermans, I am thankful for your inspiring leadership, relentless optimism, and for making change happen. Fabien Casteran, thank you for continuously finding opportunities for growth—your creativity and positive attitude move mountains. Florence Mottay, thank you for giving me my first job in the Netherlands, and for taking every opportunity you have to teach me and help me grow.

Caroline Wong, thank you so much for showing me the strength and the tremendous power of being vulnerable. Ksenia Peguero, you always reach heights that I thought were impossible. Thank you for being such an inspiring reference to me and to everyone around you. You make the world a better place. Gabriele Guiseppini, *grazie* for being an amazing mentor in my early software security days (and who became a friend for life). Paco Hope, thank you for being a great mentor who tirelessly helped me grow.

To my wonderful group of close friends, I am thankful for your support over the years: Jonas Alves, Tito Araya, Pedro Calado, Gustavo Carvalho, Francisco Delgado, Sunil Dixit, Šejla Dmitrović, Monica Ercolano, Isménia Estríbio, Flávio Geraldes, Ricardo Inglês, Liz and Camilhe, Pere Mas, Ellen Moar, Ritesh Sinha, Avi Steinberg, Rachel and Estragon Stewart, Bjorn Verhelst, and Frederik Vermeesch.

I have been tremendously lucky to have met, worked with, and been inspired by stunning thought leaders in our industry. I am very thankful for everything you have taught me and that I learned from you: Ivo van den Berg, Lalit Bhakuni, Carin Biemond, Hugo Bongers, Alexandra Caraghiulea, Rogier Fischer, Michael Guardiola, Cengiz Han Sahin, Yasmine de Jeu, Annemieke Kemp, Martin Knobloch, Dr. Robbert Kramer, Hoi-Thien Man, Dr. Gary McGraw, Remko Mens, Jacqueline Nijzink, Steven Raspe, Raviv Raz, Dennis de Reus, Irfaan Santoe, Lydia van Schaik, Sabine Schmidt, Rajiv Sinha, Pieter Smallegange, and Niels Vink, just to name a few.

I would like to extend my gratitude to a wonderful set of people who make work exciting, fun, and challenging. I appreciate every one of you:

For bonuses go to ...

Mo Ahajjam, Dr. Lampis Alevizos, Shairesh Algoe, Jagmeet Arora (for your inspiring ambition), Ruben Balk, Eduardo Bárbaro, Biswajit Behera, Tom van den Berg, Joel Blaauw (for showing me kindness is contagious), Folkert de Boer, Eugene Braginets, Tanya Compton, Elvir Crnic, Eng. Adriana Sofia Dias, Evelyn van Dijk (for your unwavering optimism), Martin Dimovski, Jeroen Franse, Dmitry Galkin, Abhishek Goel, Lars Gotte, Stefan Groot, Suyi Guo, Ayhan Gunduz, Lien Haarlemmer, Sophie Haverkamp, Michiel Hilders, Ramses van Hooft, Tom Hoogendijk, Brenda van het Hul, Ingrid Icke, Rini Icent, Nilo Kambiz, Mark and Neeti Kazemier, Michel Kempes, Saghar Khadem, Nick Kirtley, Bernard Knaapen, Alexa Krayenhoff (for your open heart), Ernst Kriek, Farisa Kuhn, Roger Lagarde, Bastiaan van de Lagemaat, Marjon Leggedoor, Pepijn Lewis, Daphne Ma, Rada Machluf, Anne Madoc, Mathijs Mons, Timo Muller, Rob Muris, Bini Oudt, Pravat Pasayat, Michiel van de Pol (for your constant support), Viola van de Pol, Dennis Postma, Anna Prudnikova, Nikki Pruijmboom, Coen Raemaekers, Marlous van Riel, Harld Röling, Erwin Saasen, Pavle Sazdov, Jeiel Schalkwijk, Robin Schouten, Chey Seur, Anne Somsen, Olaf Streutker (for your service to your colleagues and society), Yunus Sultani, Rob Thiehatten, Elli Tsiala, Christos Tziotzios, Richard Verbrugge, Vincent Verhaar, Nikkie Visser, Mark Wiggerman (I am lucky to have learned from you, and everyone around you is lucky to learn from you), Ayhan Yavuz (for your inspiring consistency and strong work ethic—we need more people like you), and for that one person whose name I forgot to write (you know who you are).

A special thank you to my team: Arie Morren, Claire Bezuidenhout, Daan Ploos van Amstel, Damon Rafieian, Emma van der Grijp, Janou Hoek, Karina Karapetyan, Kemal Yesilbek, Mark Ottema, Neda Ahmadi, Nikos

Stratigos, Raj Bhalwankar, Sander Oerlemans, Sunny Zichterman, Supriya Tripathi, Suzan Versnel, Vincent Cai, Vitali Burla, and Yulia Bobrovnikova. You're the best! Thank you.

Arnaud's Acknowledgements: I am fortunate to have an amazing extended family. To my parents, aunts, uncles, cousins, and the Closel and Wiehe family, you have all been an incredible source of inspiration, love, and support. To have such amazing role models is truly a gift. I love and thank you all.

To Mom, Dad, Dave, and my siblings Jerome, Sarah, and Isabelle, you have been by my side and witnessed me through all the stages of my life. I could not have asked for a more kind, generous, and loving family. I am so grateful for the love, acceptance, and encouragement that you give me. In your company, I am truly myself and feel loved and respected.

To some of my dearest friends, Brett McDougall, Dmitry Badiarov, Rina Smith, Yvette Mommsen, and Frances-Marie Uitti, thank you for inspiring me and for all the wonderful memories.

I would like to extend my gratitude to all my FedEx colleagues (too many to mention individually), who have been an immense source of support and inspiration throughout my career. Your unwavering encouragement, guidance, and feedback have been invaluable in shaping me. You have contributed to my professional growth. Your expertise, dedication, and passion have been a constant source of motivation and have pushed me to strive for excellence in all that I do.

To Tiago, my wonderful co-author, thanks for pushing me to start a second book. While I wasn't yet ready to start on this journey, you were the catalyst that I needed. Writing this book with you has been a rewarding and enjoyable experience. I have learned a great deal from your experience, research, and wisdom.

About the Authors

Tiago Teles is an internationally recognized keynote speaker, lecturer, and author. He is a highly accomplished MBA graduate and certified CISSP professional with a wealth of experience in cybersecurity, with over 20 years of experience. He has spent several years leading security operations within banks, managing the development of security strategies to protect financial data and resources from malicious actors. With an extensive background in risk management, auditing, and compliance, Tiago is well-equipped to develop robust security measures that meet the highest industry standards.

Arnaud Wiehe is the author of the award-winning book, *The Book on Cybersecurity*. He is also a keynote speaker, consultant, and highly experienced cybersecurity leader with over 20 years of experience. He has worked in leadership cybersecurity roles for some of the largest companies in the world. He holds several prestigious cybersecurity certifications, including Certified Information Systems Security Professional (CISSP), Certified Cloud Security Professional (CCSP), Certified Information Security Manager (CISM), Certified Information Systems Auditor (CISA), and Certified Fraud Examiner (CFE).

Throughout his career, Arnaud has demonstrated a strong focus on security best practices and a keen interest in emerging trends and technologies. He is widely respected by his peers as an expert in security strategy, risk management, and governance, and is frequently called upon to speak at conferences and consult with his employers.